The Book of Gins and Vodkas

The Book of Gins and Vodkas

A Complete Guide

BOB EMMONS

OPEN COURT
Chicago and La Salle, Ilinois

To order books from Open Court, call toll-free 1-800-815-2280.

Open Court Publishing Company is a division of Carus Publishing Company.

Copyright © 2000 by Carus Publishing Company

First printing 2000

Printed and bound in the United States of America.

Cover photo © Thom Lang/The Stock Market
Interior drawings by Sara Swan

Library of Congress Cataloging-in-Publication Data

Emmons, Bob, 1940–
    The book of gins and vodkas : a complete guide / Bob Emmons.
        p.   cm.
    Includes bibliographical references and index.
    ISBN 0-8126-9410-4 (cloth : alk. paper)
    1. Gin. 2. Vodka.   I. Title.
    TP607.G4E46   1999
    641.2'55—dc21   99-38887
                                                                      CIP

Contents

Preface

There was a time when both gin and vodka were rarities in the United States. Then gin, widely-imbibed because of Prohibition, became the basis of the martini, which ruled the roost among cocktails before it was eventually ousted by the margarita. Vodka took longer to become popular, also as the foundation for cocktails, but eventually vodka outranked gin in the cocktail pecking order.

Today vodka is the biggest part of the United States distilled spirits market, accounting for 24.78 percent of sales. Gin has 8.57 percent. So together they account for over a third of the sales of spirits.

Recently, both gin and vodka have shared in the general fate of the liquor industry: declining overall sales, accompanied by a growing demand for the superior and usually more expensive labels, called 'super-premiums' by industry insiders. This rise of the superior and more expensive product, which is obviously related to our long-term rise in real incomes, first showed itself with the single-malt scotches, then with the single-barrel or small-batch bourbons, and then the 100-percent *agave* tequilas. Now the trend is well under way with vodkas, most conspicuously in such Polish imports as Chopin and Belvedere. The trend is just beginning with gins, exemplified in such labels as Bombay Sapphire, Tanqueray Malacca, Leyden, and (at over $100 per bottle) Kennsington.

There is also right now a renewed interest in gins and vodkas among young people, and a resuscitation of formerly declining cocktails like the martini, associated with the Swing revival and the lounge-hopping scene.

For those people who wonder just what the differences are among different styles of vodkas and gins, or who want to know how they can tell a good gin or vodka from an indifferent one, this book provides all the necessary information. It explains what gins and vodkas are and how they're made, gives a survey of the many different varieties and labels, explains a little about their history, and provides expert tasting notes on all the most important labels.

Along with the proliferation of new brands of vodka, some of them from the former Communist countries, there is the rapidly-growing sector of flavored vodkas, embodying all the flavors of the tastebud spectrum, from chocolate to bison grass. Strictly speaking, gin is also a flavored vodka—flavored with a special group of herbs and spices called 'botanicals', with one botanical, juniper berry, always predominating.

In this book, I also describe other drinks in the vodka family: the schnappses, aquavits (or akavits, or akvavits), vodka liqueurs, and genevers, and I say a little about drinks that are really vodkas, though distilled from sugarcane or rice. Most vodkas, of course, are distilled from corn, wheat, or rye, but some interesting exceptions are made from potatoes.

I was encouraged to write *The Book of Gins and Vodkas* by the very warm reception of *The Book of Tequila*. Like that earlier book, *The Book of Gins and Vodkas* goes much more deeply than other books into providing information and conveying a real understanding of these kinds of drinks.

When writing *The Book of Tequila*, I was often asked why I would want to write a book about tequila, and my answer was always the same: 'Because there isn't one!' The exact same question was asked about *The Book of Gins and Vodkas*, and I replied in exactly the same way: 'Because there isn't one!' There had been a number of books about both kinds of drinks, but they were almost always very short, superficial, and factually inaccurate.

While I was working on *The Book of Gins and Vodkas*, two books appeared which do contain reliable information: *Classic Vodka* by Nicholas Faith and Ian Wisniewski (Prion Books, 1997) and *The Vodka Companion: A Connoisseur's Guide* by Desmond Begg (Running Press, 1998). Both are worth reading, but are more like small picture books, covering the subject of vodka in less depth than I do, and without covering gin.

I sincerely hope that you can use this book to get more pleasure out of life. Na zdrovya!

Acknowledgments

This book would have been impossible without the information provided by and the assistance of the various companies in the liquor industry in the United States. Their help in gathering the information needed was invaluable.

Special thanks go to the various import companies that provided information about the history of the types of spirits discussed here, including but not limited to: Mr. David Van de Velde of Luctor International, Lori Tieszen of Finnish National Distilleries, and Lauren Nowicki of Palm Bay Imports.

The assistance of Dr. Roger Boulton of UC Davis Oenology and Viticulture Department was beyond thanks, especially when it comes to the detailed explanations of what happens inside a column still while the spirits are being made.

PART I

The
World
of
Vodkas

1
What Vodka Is

Brigitte Bardot, modern jazz, Polish vodka.

Pablo Picasso, upon being asked about the most
significant developments in French culture after
World War II

Vodka is a unique drink. It's a spirit, but quite unlike all
other spirits, with the exception of gin. As we shall see
later, gin has historical origins utterly alien to vodka, but
has evolved into what it is today: essentially a flavored
vodka.

So just what is vodka? What separates vodka from
brandy, rum, scotch, bourbon, or tequila?

These other spirits are defined by *how they are made,
where they are made, and what raw materials they are made
from.* But vodka can be made by any distillation process
that will produce a definite purity of alcohol. Vodka can
be made anywhere—and is manufactured in almost every
country. Vodka can be made from any raw materials that
will ferment, and is made today mainly from grain but
also from a wide variety of other raw materials.

With other spirits, the aim is to preserve the distinctive flavors and aromas yielded by age-old production

methods. So, with rising incomes and the desire for higher-quality liquor, there is a revolt against mass production methods where these threaten the palate and the nose. There's a return to slower, more traditional, and more troublesome procedures.

With scotch whisky, we see the decline of blends and the rise of the single malts—striking and distinctive tastes and aromas, full of history and character. With bourbon, we likewise observe the growth of the 'single-barrel' or 'small-batch' bourbons. With tequila, we can observe the growing appreciation of the very best one-hundred-percent *agave* tequilas.

With vodka, the scene is just the reverse. The historical tendency has been to eliminate just those colorful tastes and smells which distillers of other liquors are so concerned to retain. Now, don't get me wrong. There is good and bad vodka, and good vodka tastes a lot better than bad vodka. But when you taste modern vodka, even the most expensive boutique vodkas (called 'super-premium' in the liquor industry), you would only be distracted by those evocative symbols of time and place, what chemists call the 'congeners', which give character and quality to scotch, bourbon, tequila, or the finest brandies.

In recent years, vodka has shared in the influences common to all distilled spirits: a decline in total consumption, but a buoyant growth in sales of those more costly labels considered to be superior in quality. Unlike the other liquors, the super-premium vodkas do not, for the most part, represent any return to traditional methods. Some will say that this revival of traditionally crafted vodkas is still to come, but this now seems unlikely. The fact is that the vodka drinker is looking for something different.

To see one striking example, go to Poland. Poland is a country where vodka is part of the national myth. The issue of whether Poland or Russia is the historical birthplace of vodka is a constant point of contention. There is a tremendous desire, allied with patriotism, to maintain the character of the traditional Polish vodkas, though compared with the character of a fine cognac or tequila, this character is itself a minutely nuanced affair. Yet if you talk to young Poles, the entrepreneurs and the intelligentsia of the capitalist renaissance in that country, you find that they want Smirnoff, they want Finlandia! They praise these foreign vodkas for their clean, fresh, flavor and aroma, which, from another point of view could be described as their comparative lack of distinctive flavor and aroma.

Anywhere, and from Anything!

Most drinks are defined, even legally defined, by what they are made *from*. Brandy has to be made from fruit, either of the tree or of the vine. Rum can only be made from sugar beets or sugarcane, either raw juice or molasses, the leftover residue from the sugar production process. Tequila is made from the juice of the blue agave. Whiskey is made from grain, and, for example, bourbon is made predominantly from corn.

How is vodka defined? The Bureau of Alcohol, Tobacco, and Firearms defines vodka as "a colorless, odorless, tasteless product of which the only ingredients are ethyl alcohol and water." Actually, it's not quite that simple. The BATF really means that the other ingredients are present in extremely minute quantities.

By law, scotch can only be made in Scotland, tequila only in Mexico, cognac only in France, and bourbon only in the United States. Vodka can be made anywhere. The very few political entities on this planet where there is no legal manufacture of vodka are generally places where some fundamentalist religious group with intemperate anti-alcohol views has seized power.

In Mongolia there are few farms and little agriculture. The entire life of the population, descendents of the nomadic Mongols, revolves around their livestock, especially their horses. On these immense open plains there are very few trees or vines.

The Mongolians produce vodka! How do they do it? For thousands of years the Mongols have drunk a fermented product called *kumiss*, made from mares' milk.

They also use this alcoholic *kumiss* as the base to distill into a vodka. I have not tasted this Mongolian vodka, but it is a certainty that the difference in taste between it and the first vodka you pick up in a U.S. liquor store will be far less than the difference between any two single-malt scotches.

Vodka is, worldwide, by far the most widespread and most easily recognized of all spirits. It can be made from any fermentable product, including beets, potatoes, raw sugar, any of the cereal grains, fruits of tree or vine, milk, and whey. Vodka has been made from flour or even bread dough and possibly even honey. (Mead, a brewed alcoholic product made from honey, was one of the precursor alcoholic beverages produced in what eventually became the vodka region.)

Purity, Clarity, Versatility

In manufacturing a high-quality brandy, rum, tequila, scotch, or bourbon, you will aim to retain as many of the 'desirable' natural flavoring agents as possible, so you will generally use a pot still. With these drinks, use of a column still might indicate that you were more concerned about low cost than about quality.

In manufacturing high-quality vodka, however, there is little point in employing the slow and expensive, old-fashioned pot still. Some vodkas are made that way, and they are interesting, but they are unlikely to be widely emulated. The way vodkas have evolved, you will actually satisfy the connoisseur better by using a continuous-action column still, which removes more of the natural flavoring agents, leaving a cleaner, purer taste and aroma.

All vodkas are filtered through charcoal, and the charcoal imparts some flavor to the vodka. But all sorts of materials can be and are employed to remove as many flavoring elements as possible. Vodka has been filtered through everything from diamond dust to fuller's earth. If a material has the ability to grab onto a slippery congener, someone will try to use it to filter vodka. The aim of all this preoccupation with filtration is to remove congeners, minute traces of elements which would give the vodka qualities the vodka lover might judge to be distracting, irrelevant, or 'impure'.

The main motive for this emphasis on purity and clarity is, of course, that vodka is most often used as the alcoholic base for cocktails. Unlike any other of the major groups of spirits, vodka will mix with anything. Hence, we now also observe the rapid growth of flavored vodkas. There are dozens of flavors. There are even chocolate vodkas and vodkas flavored with bison grass.

And so we see that vodka generally fills a different role from other spirits. People always want a combination of interesting flavors with an alcoholic kick. The approach of other spirits has been to produce them in a way that retains the interesting flavors while distilling the alcohol. The approach of vodka is to purify and clarify the spirit, eliminating many interesting flavors, but yielding a highly versatile and adaptable product. The other flavors can then be added at will.

Yet many millions of people drink vodka straight, or almost straight. And here we arrive at the fundamental symbolic significance of vodka. The choice of an alcoholic beverage is an affirmation of one's fundamental values.

Vodka stands for purity, clarity, and the desirability of being a good mixer. The values of the vodka lover are high-tech values: efficacy and precision. The vodka drinker feels at home amid the bright lights of the big city. Whereas the lover of whiskey or tequila celebrates the virtues of village life—the unbroken rhythm of tradition and the conviviality of old acquaintances—the vodka devotee favors movement, progress, and endless experimentation.

The Universality of Vodka

As a result, vodka is the most widespread and the most easily recognized of all spirits. At this time the largest-selling single label of the vodka family on a worldwide basis is probably a Korean product labeled 'Jinro'. It is called a shochu or soju, being made in a method similar to that used to prepare the national Japanese product 'sake', a rice beer. Jinro is a distilled product which sold over 44 million cases in 1995, mainly in Asia. This particular beverage is made from rice but is manufactured by rectifying from a high-proof rice distillate which fills all the requirements of being a vodka. The product is marketed at a low 48 proof and has sugar and citric acid added to make it a kind of citrus liqueur, though the flavors are not strong enough to make much impression. It is surprisingly neutral in flavor and aroma.

The sales level of this drink may surprise some because Russia is popularly supposed to be the largest consumer of vodka, and in 1997 still consumed two billion quarts of vodka, or about 200,000,000 nine-liter cases, but outside of Russia, Jinro has sold the most cases of any individual brand.

But vodka is also made in every country in Europe, most areas in Latin America, and many other countries on all continents except Antarctica. It is even made in the Philippines and Thailand.

Most of the Polish vodkas are made from rye, barley, or potatoes; Russian vodkas are usually made from rye or wheat. The vodkas from Sweden are usually wheat or grain-mixture distillates which are mostly wheat. Finland's 'Finlandia' vodka has always used six-row barley as the only base material for its vodka, but many other countries routinely use wheat or rye. Belgium and the low countries make a lot of vodka from molasses left over from the sugar beet conversion process which yields table sugar. In England many of the vodkas are made from corn (what the British call 'maize'), but on the European continent most vodkas use mainly a combination of wheat and rye.

Other styles of vodkas are made in the areas of the world where they grow sugar cane, because the sugar crystallization process leaves behind the fermentable raw material called molasses. It is usually the base product of the spirit known as rum, but if it is distilled at a high enough proof level and filtered through charcoal, it will serve as a vodka. At least one of the rum companies is making a product that they are marketing to serve as both spirits. Bacardi-Martini makes a product called 'Exclusiv', which they market around the world as either a vodka or a light rum.

Along with the vodkas, there are also similar spirits made in Europe, Akavit or Aquavit, which is a grain spirit from the Baltic region, and Schnapps from Germany. Both are vodka-style spirits, and schnapps is normally a flavored product, especially in the U.S., though in Europe the product is made as an unflavored spirit and marketed much as are vodkas. Aquavit is also a grain based spirit, always flavored with caraway seeds.

The fastest-growing trend in the vodka category of distilled spirits market is the flavored vodka portion, with one company from England (Black Death), having 24 different flavors of vodka on the market in the U.K..

There is even a black vodka, Blavod's 'Original Black Vodka', which is colored by an obscure Burmese herb called 'Black Cacheau'. This is a jet-black vodka which pales slightly to a greyish-black when mixed with a diluting agent such as your standard drink mixer. When mixed with orange juice, however, it turns green. The company assures you that the vodka will not stain your teeth black, and in England, it has gone from an idea to the third-largest selling vodka in that country in only one year. Although it's a perfectly good vodka, the main force driving its sales appears to be its new and highly unusual appearance: young people can feel re-assured that 'Daddy never drank it'.

Vodka is truly the spirit which mixes with other flavors more readily than any other. Though gin may have been the first product to be used in the making of mixed drinks, vodka is the spirit which has grown up in the cocktail age. Any drink that can be made with another spirit can also be made with vodka. In 1997 one national liquor company sued two other national liquor companies for making a 'margarita' with vodka or wine, rather than the original and correct tequila. The case was settled before trial in favor of the tequila side, but the fact remains that vodka can replace almost any spirit in a mixed drink without harming the flavor of the final drink. It may not taste the same as the original concoction, but it won't taste at all bad because you use vodka instead of the spirit called for in the original recipe.

It's the Water, Stupid

So while vodka can be made from anything, it mixes with all other ingredients to make a cocktail. To a chemist, vodka is overwhelmingly just water, alcohol, and trace amounts of carbon. This makes the water used for the dilution process very important to the final taste of the vodka. Since water is about 60 percent of a bottle of 80 proof vodka, the water is a very important ingredient indeed. Russians sometimes claim that the soft 'living' water from their rivers and lakes is what makes their vodkas better than those produced in other areas of the world. Some producers from other countries may question this assertion, but the Russians insist it is 'pravda' (truth).

Most U.S. domestic vodkas use distilled water for their dilution, though some do use spring water, and others use softeners to give the water a pure characteristic. In Europe, one of the Polish distilleries actually had a Culligan water purification system installed to purify and soften all of the water from their deep well and this is the water they use to dilute their vodka.

Finlandia vodka from Primalco, owned by the Finnish government, uses water from underground rivers that flow through the rocks of the Arctic moraine. They state that this water is among the purest on Earth; it is basically spring water arising from melting glaciers. There is a vodka made in Canada called 'Iceberg', which uses glacial ice to make their spirit. They actually have boats that pick up chunks of icebergs and bring them back to the distillery where they are melted and used to dilute the product. Since most glacial ice was laid down thousands or even tens of thousands of years ago, they may have some claim to be using one of the purest waters available for any vodka label.

Types of Vodka

The first major division of vodkas is into flavored and non-flavored vodkas. Then, vodka can be classified according to the material used to ferment and distill alcohol. Most vodka is made from grain, so the big division here is into grain and non-grain sources of spirits. Although the differences in taste are subtle and elusive, a good taster can usually tell immediately whether a vodka has been made from materials other than grain. For instance, excellent vodka is made from potatoes, and these vodkas have a characteristic silkiness of flavor and texture. Vodka made from sugarcane has a distinctly raisiny feel.

If we focus our attention, then, on non-flavored vodkas made from grain, the big division is between the 'traditional' Polish and Russian vodkas on the one hand, and Western vodkas, on the other. Generally, Western vodkas have gone further down the path of purity, clarity, and elimination of distinctive or traditional congeners. The Polish and Russian vodkas may therefore be considered the 'traditional' vodkas. In Russia, each distillery makes everything from scratch, mainly from wheat, with some rye. In Poland there are around 450 regional distilleries which sell their grain spirit to 25 'polmoses' or rectifying companies. Most Polish grain spirit is produced from rye, with some wheat. Barley and potatoes are also sometimes used in producing Polish vodka, but currently not Russian vodka.

When all of these facts are considered, it becomes obvious that many of the products that we consume as vodka, are in reality not quite what we are brought to expect. In Poland, some may be surprised that the normal process includes buying high-proof spirit from a large group of regional distilleries which make alcohol at about 180 proof for the specific purpose of selling it to the main rectification plants now called 'polmoses'.

When Poland was still under the rule of the Communist government, all aspects of vodka production were owned and controlled by the state. At that time the smaller regional distilleries, the polmoses, and the marketing arm, Agros Trading, were all owned and controlled by the central government.

Today, after the rise of capitalism and democracy in Poland, all of the polmoses are separate companies, though most still work in concert with each other and allow Agros Trading to market their products. Agros does retain control of many of the brands known to be Polish vodkas, and because of that has managed to keep control of the marketing and exporting for most of the polmos rectification plants.

Currently two distilleries in Poland are operating independently from Agros. They are the Polmos Siedlce which makes 'Chopin', and the Bols-Unicoop distillery in Oborniki. All the others can make and market new products independent of Agros, but are continuing to cooperate in the manufacture of most vodkas. Only the new super-premium labels that the polmos distilleries have developed for export are free from the restrictions imposed by Agros; all others are still controlled by that agency. And in Poland, the polmos distilleries are forbidden to advertise their products, so their best bet is to export.

Western vodkas can be broadly divided into those produced in the U.S., Europe, and the rest of the world, though these are all produced by essentially the same standard method. So many vodkas are made and marketed in the U.S. by companies called 'rectifiers' that there are actually more vodkas made in the U.S. than those that are imported into the U.S. from other countries.

Nearly all U.S. vodkas are manufactured in the standard Western method, that is with potable neutral grain spirits (usually made from number 2 yellow corn, the main type of grain available in the midwest), distilled by and purchased from one of the major grain processing companies. There are four of these companies in the U.S, three with their home offices in Illinois, and one in Kansas.

These four companies make at least 99 percent of the potable grain spirits used to make vodka in the U.S. The standard method of production by the vodka companies is to purchase the alcohol at very high proof, always at 190 proof or higher, looking for the highest purity of alcohol that can be maintained in a non-airtight container. Alcohol has a chemical attraction for water and if left in any sort of non airtight vessel will absorb water from the surrounding atmosphere until it reaches the approximate level of 191.5 proof or 95.75 percent alcohol.

After receiving the neutral grain spirits in the processing plant, the rectifier filters the spirit, dilutes it to bottle strength, bottles, labels, and ships it for sale. Regional rectification companies sell this product to many other companies for use under their own private labels. Most grocery and drug store chains purchase the spirit, and have the rectifier bottle and label it with their own brands to sell in their retail stores. This is where the store brands of vodkas come from.

So in the United States, this is what you drink when you purchase a bottle of domestic vodka. The imports are handled a little differently, since some of them do make their own neutral grain spirit from scratch. Some countries such as Finland, Germany, and Sweden follow monopolistic practices in which the government owns all distillation facilities. So these governments watch the product very carefully and exert complete control over it from beginning to end. Germany makes the neutral grain spirit and then sells it to rectification companies, while Finland and Sweden own and manage the entire process.

Other countries and companies do not follow this plan but use practices similar to those followed in the U.S., where high-proof spirit is purchased from other companies which do the distillation and the buyer then alters the spirit into the desired product.

In the U.S., I have found only three vodka producers who make their own neutral grain spirit. Seagram's, of course, makes neutral grain spirit since their grain processing center supplies potable alcohol for all of their alcohol processes. But Seagram's doesn't make or market a domestic vodka. They exclusively import and market all of the products of V & S Vin and Spirits of Sweden,

Tito Beveridge, with his trusty 'Dog-Jo', in front of his
old-fashioned pot still, where he makes 'Tito's Handmade Vodka'.
It's a remarkably good vodka, but what's even more remarkable,
some would say, is simply to find a legal distillery in Texas.

the government owned maker of 'Absolut' and the new
super-premium vodka, 'Sundsvall'.

The other three domestic vodkas manufactured from
scratch are 'Teton Glacier Potato Vodka', made outside
Rigby, Idaho from processed potatoes; 'Rain', a vodka
made entirely from organic corn grown at Fizzle Flat
Farm, in Yale, Iowa, and processed and distilled at the
Leestown   distillery   in   Frankfort,   Kentucky,   and

'Exclusiv', a sugarcane-based spirit manufactured by Bacardi-Martini in their plant in San Juan, Puerto Rico, and marketed as either a vodka or a very light rum. All other vodkas made in the United States are made in the manner I have described as 'standard'.

In Europe, many vodkas are also made from purchased spirit, and in certain instances re-distilled to the parameters of the manufacturer. Many of the British vodkas are made in this way, since British law forbids the making of gin on the same premises where neutral grain spirits are made. While the relationship between vodka and the gin companies may seem obscure, many of the English gin makers also make vodka, or perhaps it's the other way around: most of the vodka makers also make gin. In England, gin came before vodka and the companies that began their businesses making gin now also make vodka. This means that many of the facilities that do make vodka in England started life as gin companies, and as such are not inclined to go to any more effort to make vodka than is used in the manufacture of gin. So they purchase neutral grain spirit and modify it into vodka, normally just by charcoal filtration.

In all the world, except Russia and Poland, the standard or 'Western' method is the one commonly used to make vodka.

GENUINE · SUPERIOR QUALITY

SKOL.

VODKA

FAMOUS SINCE 1849

IOWA REFUND 5¢

DISTILLED FROM GRAIN · I
J.A. DOUGHERTY'S SONS, CO
OWENSBORO, KENT
0 85676 10110 7   40.3% ALC/VOL (80.6 PROOF) · PI

MR. BOSTON'S®

Riva
VODKA

40% ALC/VOL (EIGHTY PROOF)
100% GRAIN NEUTRAL SPIRITS
BOTTLED BY MR. BOSTON DISTILLER
OWENSBORO, KY., ALBANY, GA

Crystal
Palace
VODKA
DISTILLED
40% ALC./VOL.   (80 PROOF)

MADE FROM 100% GRA
BOTTLED BY BARTO
BARDSTOWN, KY., LOS,

EXTRA DRY

Bentley's®

genuine
VODKA

40% ALC./VOL. (80 PROOF)
100% GRAIN NEUTRAL SPIRITS
PRODUCT OF U.S.A.
BOTTLED BY
Oak Park Distilling Co.
BALTIMORE, MD.

FINEST DELUXE QUALITY

RIKALOFF

VODKA

100% GRAIN NEUTRAL SPIRITS
40% ALC. BY VOL. (80 PROOF)
BOTTLED BY
NTAL DISTILLING CO., BALTIMORE, MARYLAND
PRODUCT OF U.S.A.

ODESSE
VODKA

PRODUCT OF U.S.A.   ALC. 40% BY VOL. (80 PROOF)

2
How Vodka Is Made

The excellence of every art must consist in the complete accomplishment of its purpose.

Benjamin Franklin

Vodka is basically water and neutral spirit, with a little carbon in the form of charcoal, and should normally contain very few impurities, even those 'impurities' which in other distilled drinks would be viewed as desirable flavoring elements.

The neutral spirit is made from any fermentable sugar source, or any starch compound which can be converted or transformed into sugar. If it's made from grain it's called neutral grain spirit, from sugarcane, neutral cane spirit, and so on.

Most vodkas are processed from one of the fermentable sugar compounds derived from grain. In the U.S. the grain is usually corn or wheat. Yeast is added to a solution of the sugar compounds in water, and the biochemical process known as fermentation then allows the yeast to convert the sugar in the solution into alcohol and carbon dioxide gas.

Grains of all types can be used to make neutral spirit, which the chemist knows as ethyl alcohol or ethanol.

The process of fermentation is basically the same whether the ultimate product is to be vodka, beer, or whiskey. There is usually some sort of helpful intervention to convert the starches inside the kernels of grain into fermentable sugars. In some beer and whiskey making processes, the grain is moistened so that it starts to sprout. When the grain sprouts, it releases a natural enzyme called maltose which converts the starch inside the grain kernel into malt sugar. The sprouting process is then halted by drying the grain, cleaning it and grinding it up into a fine meal or grist, which is cooked in water and allowed to cool. The liquid containing the sugar can then either be separated from the grain residue or left throughout the fermentation process. After cooling, yeast is added to the mixture to begin fermentation.

If the sprouting process has not been employed, some other method of starch conversion must be used. Normally the grain, after having been thoroughly cleaned, is ground up and cooked to form a mash. Amylase or diastase (other enzymes closely related to maltose) will be added to the mash, after it has cooled, to trigger the conversion to sugar. When all of the starch has been converted to sugar, the yeast will be added just as in the earlier method and fermentation will occur.

Ideally, fermentation should convert 100 pounds of sugars into 51 pounds of carbon dioxide gas and 49 pounds of alcohol, but this is a best-case scenario that happens only theoretically. Usually, in any solution ready for fermentation, there are many other products which do not completely convert. So we will normally get less than the above proportions of alcohol and carbon dioxide, because some more or less inert material in the solution do not undergo the changes associated with fermentation.

In the process of fermentation, many things happen, and very small differences in the base ingredients or in the process itself can cause big changes in the flavor or aroma of the final product. One important factor which may affect the taste and nose of the product is the use of accelerants or yeast foods. These additives cause fermentation to proceed much faster than it would naturally do. If the fermentation process is allowed to proceed at the normal rate found in nature, it will take a week to ten days to convert all of the sugar into alcohol and carbon dioxide gas, depending on the climate, weather and temperature at the time fermentation occurs. If accelerants are used, the process can be cut to a day or less. These additives allow the yeasts to divide and consume the sugars much faster, and the by-products are also formed much faster than normal. Accelerants are usually compounds of nitrogen: in olden days the most common additives were urea or saltpeter.

After fermentation, there will normally be impurities such as alcohols other than ethyl alcohol, as well as esters and aldehydes, included in the final product. A modern column still will remove the majority of these chemical impurities though some will be left in the product, even after distillation. Some of these components contribute aromas and flavors to the finished product that may be either pleasant or unpleasant, and it can be tricky to predict which you're going to get. Most modern vodka companies try to remove just about as many of these impurities as possible before bottling the finished vodka.

With other distilled drinks, the aim is to eliminate the undesirable components while keeping the desirable ones. And even with the more traditional forms of vodka production, this remains an objective to some extent. Traditional manufacturers believe that the congeners remaining in the product after distillation add character and so they choose to leave some of these components in the finished product. Polish and Russian vodka producers do this as a matter of course.

Among the other components removed by the modern distillation process are fusel oils and methyl alcohol (methanol or wood alcohol), both of which can be dangerous, and are responsible for the deadly reputation of bootleg whiskey. At one time there was also the hazard that stills might be constructed using lead solders, thereby adding concentrations of highly toxic heavy metals to the liquor. All modern column stills are made with either copper or stainless steel, welded with non-toxic metals, and all the potentially dangerous components are removed as a matter of course.

Pot Stills and Column Stills

The chemical components called 'congeners' are natural flavoring agents left over from the fermentation process. Makers of fine-quality brandies, rums, tequilas, or whiskeys consider these components vital to the quality of their products, and aim to retain many of them. In such cases, pot stills are generally superior to column stills. But for those products where the clarity, purity, and mixability of the spirit is the most desired end (vodkas, gins, aquavits, and schnappses), a continuous action or column still will normally be preferred.

Pot stills allow some congeners to pass through the distillation process. It would take many distillations through a pot still to attain the same purity of spirit as a column still can achieve in one distillation. In a pot still, the fermented must is not normally heated above a temperature of 185–190 degrees Fahrenheit, and two distillations are used to achieve the intended proofages for the desired spirit. This comparatively low average temperature prevents the less volatile spirits from ever leaving the main mass of fluid in the pot. The result is that a spirit distilled in a pot still normally has more character (complexity, character, and subtlety, in the mouth and in the nose) than a spirit from a column still.

How a Column Still Works

Spirits made in a continuous action or column still are heated to a higher temperature (usually close to the boiling point of water, 212 degrees Farenheit or 100 degrees Celsius). The interior of a modern column still is laid out in such a way as to separate out the chemical components of the fermented must. There are two columns in a standard first run column still. The first is called the wash or beer column and the second is called the alcohol column.

The beer column acts much as does a pot still in that it drives the alcohol components of the fermented must or wash out of the top of the still, leaving the liquid water and any solid components to drain out of the bottom of the column. In the beer column the initial must is injected into the column at the top of the column, with the steam injected into the bottom of the column at about the boiling point of water and approximately 15 pounds per square inch pressure. As the heat passes up through the fermented material, it vaporizes out the volatile alcoholic components and they rise up the column to the top where they are drawn off and passed on to the alcohol column.

In the second column, the alcohol column, there is a series of perforated plates located near the vaporization/condensation levels of each type of alcohol within the column. The temperature varies within the column, from the highest heat and pressure at the bottom of the column to lower temperatures as you go higher up. The levels within the still where the collection plates are located are controlled by the temperature and pressure maintained within the column itself. The higher up the column you progress, the lower the internal temperature, so that the more volatile the component, the higher up the column it climbs.

The highest plate in the column is the one which would normally draw methyl alcohol or methanol out of the still. This product should not form during the regular grain fermentation process unless pectin or related fruit compounds have been fermented or placed in the fermented material. Normal production from grain, potatoes, or sugarcane does not contain the enzymes which would produce methanol. Usually only fruit-based alcohols will produce methyl alcohol during the fermentation process. This allows the top plate to be one of the main draws for the ethyl alcohol which will become neutral grain spirit. Methyl alcohol has a vaporization point of 140.5 degrees Farenheit, the lowest of any of the alcohols making it the most volatile of the different types of alcohols.

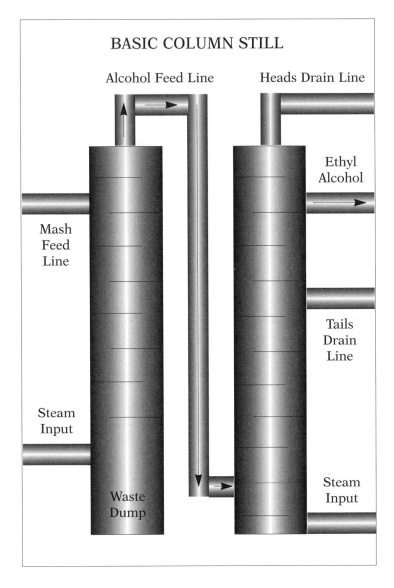

BASIC COLUMN STILL

Alcohol Feed Line

Heads Drain Line

Ethyl
Alcohol

Mash
Feed
Line

Tails
Drain
Line

Steam
Input

Steam
Input

Waste
Dump

The second plate is the one in which the distiller is usually most interested, for it is the plate which is most often used to drain ethyl alcohol or ethanol, the most desired component for any spirit which is 'potable' (fit to drink). The vaporization/condensation point of ethyl alcohol is 172.9 degrees Fahrenheit. The other alcohol components and their vaporization/condensation temperatures are: isopropyl alcohol, 180.1 degrees

Farenheit; terto-butyl Alcohol, 181 degrees Farenheit; allyl alcohol, 206 degrees Farenheit; a-propyl alcohol, 207 degrees Farenheit; secbutyl alcohol, 211 degrees Farenheit; water, 212 degrees Farenheit; isobutyl alcohol, 226.2 degrees Farenheit; a-butyl alcohol, 243.9 degrees Farenheit; isoamyl alcohol, 270 degrees Farenheit; amyl alcohol, 280 degrees Farenheit; and benzyl alcohol, 401 degrees Farenheit.

In an alcohol column, these components are usually kept down in the lower plates, but in a pot still some will pass through the distillation process, since all the alcohols clump together when being drawn from a solution. To avoid these components being in the final product, a pot still uses head and tail cuts, where only the middle 35 to 50 percent of the initial distillation run is allowed to be included in the second run. The heads are those components which vaporize first, usually methyl alcohol, and the tails are those which vaporize at a higher temperature and are drawn up the neck and removed after the heart of the run, which mainly yields the ethyl alcohol. The tails will usually be included in the mash of the next distillation run in an attempt to recover as much potable alcohol as possible.

The actual distillation in a column still occurs in a manner very similar to the rectification unit used to separate the components of crude oil into the different elements of benzene, gasoline, kerosene, naphtha, and the other higher and lower components including asphalts, tars, and other substances obtained from the petroleum cracking process.

As to the recovery plates inside the column still, they are perforated and shaped differently for different purposes. Some have a slight rise or dome in the center of the round plate and a trough running around the outside edge. As the trough fills up with the condensed element, it overflows into a drainage pipe which leads to a holding tank, or if the product is drawn off as a vapor, it goes through a condenser, is condensed into a liquid and stored. For the ethyl alcohol, it is held and readied for dilution, filtration and bottling, and the other components, 'heads' or 'tails', are held for redistillation through the other columns of the still for further alcohol recovery. Some companies simply discard the heads, since they are not usable for potable alcohol; larger companies may save them for use as motor fuel components. When a still has more than two columns, the additional columns are used only to redistill the tails to recover the potable ethyl alcohol contained therein, or in certain instances to remove aldehydes. So the actual main distillation is carried out in the first two columns, the beer column and the alcohol column, and the additional columns are used just to recover as much further alcohol as possible from the foreshots and aftershots.

For marketing purposes some vodka companies state that their product is distilled four, five, or six times. Usually this just means that the still has four, five, or six columns. But the number of columns a continuous action still has, beyond the first two, will not affect the product from the first distillation since that alcohol is never reprocessed. All the additional columns do is redistill the tails in an effort to recover any further alcohol present therein.

Exceptionally, certain companies do claim to redistill purchased neutral grain spirit to remove some impurities, but such vodka labels are very few. One such company is Fifth Generation Inc., located in Austin, Texas. This is the company which makes Tito's Handmade Vodka, currently being distributed in Texas but looking for national representation and distribution.

Unbelievable Claims About Pot Stills

Some companies even claim that their vodka is totally made in pot stills, which is a little difficult to imagine in this day and age. Before the column still was invented during the first half of the nineteenth century, all alcoholic beverages were distilled in pot stills. Today's high-efficiency column stills make this practice obsolete for vodka and the claims seem difficult to credit.

When alcohol is distilled in a pot still, there is a certain limit of how much alcohol the pot still can concentrate during a single distillation run. My friend Dr. Roger Boulton, professor of eonology and viticulture at the University of California, Davis, and one of the leading teaching professors on the art of distillation in the world today, came up with the following calculations.

If you begin with 100 liters of a solution which contains 5% alcohol in a fermented must and the must is distilled until 0.5% alcohol is left in the pot, the first distillation run will concentrate that volume of alcohol to 17 liters at 24% or 48 proof. The second distillation will further concentrate that 17 liters to 6 liters at 53% or 106 proof. The third distillation will further concentrate it to 3.5 liters at 73% or 146 proof. The fourth run through the still of the remaining 3 and one half liters will result in 2.3 liters at 83% or 166 proof, and the fifth run will further concentrate the 2.3 liters to 2 liters at 88% or 176 proof.

When you compare the results of these five runs through a pot still with a single run through a column still, it becomes pretty clear that it is, to say the very least, inefficient to use a pot still to try to make the neutral grain spirits intended for vodka. Since you must heat the liquid in the pot each time you make a distillation run, the energy costs become very significant and the purity of the final output at the end of five distillation runs remains less than that from one run through a column still.

This example makes clear that a considerable amount of alcohol is not recovered when distillation is conducted in this fashion. In 100 liters of 5% alcohol in a fermented must, there should be 5 liters of 100% pure alcohol. In this instance only 2 liters of 176 proof was recovered, a little less than 40% of the available total. Most of this missing alcohol is lost at the outset when 10% of the total is not recovered but left in the pot at the end of the distillation run. Each succeeding run loses more alcohol and additional portions are lost simply through the transfer and reheating of the product. In column stills, however, much more of the alcohol would be recovered, probably as much as 95% of the available alcohol or 4.8

liters of 191 proof, versus 2 liters of 176 proof as recovered from the five pot still distillations.

This should demonstrate that, while pot stills can serve very well to concentrate alcohol to potable strengths, especially when the aim is to preserve much of the 'character' of the drink, they're extremely inefficient when it comes to making high-purity, high-proof alcohol. Each time you redistill in a pot still the entire mash must be reheated to the vaporization point, while in the much more efficient continuous-action column still, the alcohol is stripped out of the mash on the first run and the redistillation is for the foreshots and feints ('feints' are tailshots) only.

The pot still and the column still are best suited to different purposes. The pot still seems to work best when the distiller wishes to preserve the character of the raw materials or base product; the column still works best when the objective is the purest and cleanest high-proof spirit achievable.

The Big Four U.S. Producers of Neutral Grain Spirit

Vodka is made somewhat differently in Poland and Russia, but in most of the world, including the U.S., it's made by the standard or Western method. In the United States, vodka is normally made from neutral grain, sugarcane, or potato spirits which have been produced in column stills. All but three of the U.S.-made vodkas are manufactured from neutral grain spirits produced by one of four major grain-processing companies. These four are Archer Daniels Midland, Midwest Grain Co., Grain Processing Corporation, and Seagram's.

Archer Daniels Midland (ADM), based in Decatur, Illinois, is the biggest, with five distillation plants, two of which can produce potable spirits. The largest of these plants, the one in Peoria, Illinois, is capable of producing 500,000 gallons of high-proof (over 190) spirit per day. ADM's smaller plant, in Clinton, Iowa, can produce about half that amount.

ADM told me they were building a new column still themselves, rather than commissioning another company such as Vendome Copper and Brass (a manufacturer of beer processing equipment and stills of both types), to build it. The dimensions of the new still are impressive indeed. It will be approximately 40 meters in height and 15 feet in diameter, and made from stainless steel. This is an unusually large column still.

Midwest Grain Co. has its home office and one of its two distilleries in Atchison, Kansas. The company's other plant is located in Perin, Illinois. Grain Processing Corporation is based in Muscatine, Illinois, and Seagram's has a major grain processing plant in Lawrenceburg, Illinois.

Together, these four companies supply almost all of the neutral grain spirits made in the United States. Seagram's distillery makes large quantities of neutral grain spirit for sale and for their own use, but they do not produce or market a vodka of their own. Instead they concentrate on being the U.S. importer and distributor of the Swedish vodka, Absolut.

Aside from ADM, Midwest Grain, and Grain Processing, I have found only three U.S. companies which make their own vodka from scratch. These are the makers of the brands known as 'Teton Glacier Potato Vodka', produced at the Silver Creek distillery in Rigby, Idaho; 'Rain' vodka, manufactured from special organic corn grown on the Fizzle Flat Farms property, in Yale, Illinois, and distilled and processed at the Leestown distillery in Frankfort, Kentucky (a bourbon distillery, owned by Sazerac, which also makes Ancient Age products); and 'Exclusiv', a cane spirit marketed by Bacardi-Martini as either a vodka or a light rum. 'Teton Glacier Potato Vodka' is marketed internationally by World Wide Wine and Spirits Co. in Norwood, New Jersey, 'Rain' vodka by Sazerac Company of New Orleans, Louisiana, and 'Exclusiv' by Bacardi-Martini USA of Miami, Florida.

It seems that all other vodkas made in the U.S. are manufactured from neutral grain spirits purchased from one of the Big Four. The actual process after the high-proof spirit arrives at the individual manufacturing plant differs, but the normal process is to filter the product through any of a number of different filtration materials, which will always include some type of activated charcoal filtration, but may include everything from 'diamond dust' to fullers or diamataceous earth, and may include cotton filters in addition to the other filtration materials.

Some few manufacturers claim to redistill the product in pot stills to remove impurities left by the distillation process. Very few make this claim, since most high-proof spirit has already had most of the impurities removed, but one in particular, Mr. Tito Beveridge of 'Tito's Handmade Vodka' of Austin, Texas states that he dilutes and redistills his product twice more to further purify it. By diluting the base alcohol to 100 proof, and redistilling it, he claims to remove some of the other alcohols mentioned before, which escape the columns in the big plants. By adding water to the base spirit and then redistilling, certain alcohol products that are less soluble in water than ethyl alcohol may be removed.

Most other vodkas go through a filtration process, are diluted to bottle strength, usually 80 proof, bottled, labeled, and shipped for sale. This is the way that most of the domestic vodkas you see in your favorite liquor or grocery store are manufactured.

The Standard Western Distillation Procedure

In the U.S. those manufacturing plants which do not distill their own neutral grain spirit are usually called rectifiers. Rectifiers are mainly bottling plants which also modify the spirit brought in from the large grain processing and distillation plants. If you tour a rectification plant, what you will normally see is a very large warehouse filled with cases of finished bottles ready for shipment. A small part of this area will have an automated bottling line and another storage area will contain large stainless steel tanks for the storage of bulk spirit while it is awaiting modification, being modified, or resting before bottling.

The neutral grain spirit arrives by railroad tank cars in lots of somewhere between 50,000 and 55,000 gallons per tank car. It is pumped from the railroad cars into large stainless steel vats inside the plant for processing and holding. The tank cars also serve as storage containers until they are emptied.

The neutral grain spirit is usually modified into either vodka or gin, with the vodka being charcoal filtered, and the gin having the botanicals added and being allowed to rest until ready for bottling. The product must contain at least one ounce of carbon for each 100 gallons of 100-proof spirit in order to be called 'vodka' under BATF regulations.

Imported Vodkas

Imported vodkas are made in fundamentally similar ways. In Russia, there are ten distilleries which themselves own their marketing branch, called Sojuzplodoimport, which along with other distilleries before the fall of communism was owned by the state. Of these ten distilleries, the seven most important are: the Cristall distillery in Moscow, and the distilleries in the cities of Irkutsk, Kaliningrad, Kaluga, Kursk, Samara, and St. Petersburg. All of these distilleries plus the other three in the consortium supply Sojuzplodoimport with the vodkas they market throughout the world as Russian vodka.

Most of the labels marketed by Sojuzplodoimport can be produced by any or all of these distilleries. The quality and consistency of the product can vary from distillery to distillery, especially when the sources of water and grain are different in these varied locations, which they always are. Since all of these products can be made in all of the other locations, unless otherwise specified, quality can be problematical when one vodka label is supposed to be from a particular region, area or distillery inside Russia.

Another possible problem of variation in quality is that when there are shortfalls in Russian grain output, rumor has it that neutral grain spirit is sometimes imported into Russia from the U.S. Big Four. Again according to industry rumor, the taxes due to the Russian government for this importation of spirit are not always paid in full. More seriously, however, some of the vodka imported from Russia into the U.S. may have been adulterated with Western rather than traditional neutral grain spirit.

The Polish vodkas, currently the import rage in the U.S., especially some of the super-premium vodkas in the beautiful new bottles, are for the most part manufactured in Polish distilleries called polmoses. Before the fall of Communism, these plants were all owned by the government, whose marketing arm was Agros Trading. Since 1989, the firms have become independent but they do in some cases still function as a group. They all manufacture brands that are owned collectively by all the companies. These include the labels 'Extra Zytnia', 'Krupnik', 'Luksosowa', 'Pieprzówka', 'Wyborowa', and 'Zubrowka' (the vodka flavored with bison grass), among others.

In Poland, 450 or so small agricultural distilleries supply already distilled spirit to the polmoses. These small distilleries process all different types of vegetable material, from all of the different types of grains to some that process only potatoes or only rye. Most of the spirit comes into the polmoses at about 170 proof and is rectified by high-quality column stills to the standard proof supplied of over 190 proof or over 95 percent alcohol. This spirit is then diluted, filtered, and bottled for sale, unless it is intended to be used for products other than vodka.

Some of the polmos distilleries do make other types of vodkas, even producing an aged vodka called 'Starka', which can sometimes be stored for as long as 50 years in oak barrels. Because it is made from cereal grains and spends years in the wood, it has a certain likeness to American bourbon or straight whiskey. At least one company has tried to bring Starka into the U.S., but this is currently being blocked by the BATF on the grounds that Starka cannot meet the definition of vodka as being odorless, colorless, and tasteless.

The new super-premium labels are being produced by individual polmoses. There are 25 of the old polmos distilleries still operating in Poland, but only a few companies are opening new distilleries. The first of these was the distillery at Obornicki which is owned by a private distiller called Unicom and is producing vodka in a joint venture with the Bols group from Holland. Many of the old polmoses are modernizing and beginning production of new and exciting products.

New European super-premium vodkas come out at the rate of almost one a month. Some of these new labels will survive but some will not. Of those currently considered new super-premiums are the labels, 'French Alps' and 'Grey Goose', both from France, the new Ukrainian vodka 'Old Kiev', a new vodka called 'Charodei' made in Belarus, V & S Vin and Spirits's new 'Sundsvall' vodka, the Italian super-premium 'Mezzaluna', and who knows how many others. The British black vodka 'Blavod' was put on the market in 1998 and has now become available in the United States.

And then there are the old stand-by imports like 'Absolut' from Sweden (the largest selling import), 'Finlandia' from Finland, Holland's 'Ketel 1' vodka, the re-birth of Russia's 'Kremlovskaya', the 24 flavors of England's 'Black Death' vodka, and innumerable other entries into the international vodka chase.

From the U.S.A., besides the new 'Teton Glacier Potato Vodka' and 'Rain' vodka, there is one of the hottest brands on the market, 'Skyy Vodka', the rage in the cobalt blue bottle. It is claimed to be the cleanest vodka on the market and the spirit is certainly among the most neutral in aroma and flavor that I have been able to find.

There is a growing range of choice among vodka labels from many countries, and many more new vodkas, some more exciting than others, will appear in the years ahead. Armed with the information provided in this book, you'll be able to separate the marketing hypebole from the reality, and be able to distinguish real differences in quality.

Remember that you are the final judge of your own preferences. As you begin to educate yourself about the world of vodka and the world of gin, you can learn what to look for, but only you can be the ultimate arbiter of your own taste. Though the better vodkas are often the more expensive, this is definitely not always the case, so you will probably want to watch out for price as well as quality.

3
Vodkas of the World

The difficulty in life is the choice

George Moore

There are hundreds of liquor companies that manufacture or market thousands of gins and vodkas. While some of these producers are located in the traditional vodka areas of Eastern Europe such as Poland, Russia, and the Baltic nations, there are many more in other parts of the world.

Since the break-up of the U.S.S.R., many distilleries in its former member states and satellite countries have continued to export alcoholic products from formerly state-owned, but now private, distilleries. These companies are often still run by the same management teams as were in charge under the previous regime.

Besides the traditional areas of Poland and Russia, some of the largest companies in terms of sales are in the Far East, with the largest-selling single brand in the world being 'Jinro', a vodka made from rice and sold throughout Asia with 1995 sales of over 44,000,000 nine-liter cases. This product can occasionally be found in the U.S. market, in a green, most often 375-ml, bottle with a red cap and a yellow and red label.

There are many other spirits which can qualify as vodkas, created from diverse raw materials. The largest alcohol distillery in the world at present is located in Thailand, making only whiskey, and there are many distilleries in Latin America that make products from sugarcane derivatives which could be called either rums or vodkas. While there are few gins made in these regions of the world, there are many rectified spirits that could be classified as vodkas, even though they are called by other names in their respective areas, such as aguardiente in Latin America and Soju in Asia.

No listing exists for all vodkas worldwide, and I shall not attempt to compile such a list in this chapter, but what follows is a more complete survey than you will find anywhere else. I have tried to include all vodkas readily available in the U.S. The U.S. is one of the world's major vodka-producing countries; most vodka consumed here is produced here.

I give the U.S. vodkas first, followed by European vodkas, then a few of the more important vodkas from the rest of the world. I list the U.S. vodkas alphabetically by company (vodka producers, then vodka importers), the others alphabetically by country.

American-made Vodkas

The companies listed below are 'rectifiers'. They buy neutral grain spirit from the manufacturers and process it to make vodka. The actual manufacturers of distilled spirits are the companies that own and run distilleries. As explained in Chapter 2, around 99 percent of all the neutral spirit used to make vodka in the U.S. is produced by the Big Four: Archer Daniels Midland, Midwest Grain, Grain Processing, and Seagram's, all located in the grain belt of the Midwest. Numerous other American companies do operate distilleries, for everything from brandies to whiskeys, and some small portion of the output of these distilleries may take the form of neutral grain spirits and occasionally find its way into vodka.

I've only been able to find three vodka companies which distill their own spirit from scratch: Silver Creek distillery, in Rigby, Idaho, which makes 'Teton Glacier Potato Vodka', the Leestown distillery owned by Sazerac Company, who make 'Rain' vodkas for that company, and the Bacardi-Martini distillery which makes 'Exclusiv'. The Bacardi distillery is actually located in San Juan, Puerto Rico, but I have included it as a domestic product since the home offices of Bacardi are in Miami, Florida, and Puerto Rico is a U.S. territory. The Leestown distillery is located in Frankfort, Kentucky.

These seven plants, then, are the only distillation plants in the United States that produce the neutral spirit which is the prime ingredient of gins and vodkas. There are a couple of plants in Canada which may posssibly also be manufacturers: the company which makes 'Iceberg' vodka, and the company which makes 'Inferno' vodka, the round bottle with the two red peppers in the vodka.

Barton Brands

This company makes all of its gins and vodkas by the standard rectification process of purchasing neutral spirits and converting them into the product desired. They currently make and distribute nationally ten gin labels and eleven vodka labels.

Bendistillery

It has been claimed that this very small company located in Bend, Oregon, and operated by the Bendis family, makes its own spirit from scratch entirely in its own pot still. Having made various enquiries and spoken with the operator and owner, Mr. Jim Bendis, I conclude that Bendistillery may redistill purchased spirit, but does not actually ferment and make its own spirit from scratch.

Currently this company is marketing about 600 nine-liter cases per year for both spirits, 'Crater Lake' vodka and 'Crystal Mountain' gin, both available only in Oregon.

Black Prince Distillery

This New Jersey–based company is a subsidiary of Star Industries of Syosset, NY, and has announced release of a new vodka labeled 'Argent'.

David Sherman Corporation

This firm, headquartered in St. Louis, Missouri, makes and markets a number of different products, but currently has two vodkas on the market, the new 'Everclear' vodka and 'Tvarski', #20 in U.S. sales, with 1997 sales of 210,000 cases.

Duggan's Distillers Products

This New Jersey–based company both makes and imports beverages that may be found across the U.S. Currently their main imported vodka is 'Cardinal', a Dutch product made from sugarbeet molasses and available both in 80 proof in a white wasp-waisted bottle and 90 proof in a black bottle of the same shape. This company has close ties with Frank-Lin Distiller's Products of San Jose.

Fifth Generation Inc.

This small company in Austin, Texas, is owned and managed by Tito Beveridge and makes only one product, 'Tito's Handmade' vodka. The spirit is purchased from Midwest Grain and run through two further pot still distillations after having been diluted with water. This process is an attempt to remove any congeners or other alcohols which may be left after the original distillation process.

The product has been well received and is well thought of in Texas, where it has sold about 2,000 cases since its inception. Tito is currently working on turning it into a nationally available brand.

Frank-Lin Distiller's Products

This San Jose, California, company is a major player on the West Coast. They currently make and market numerous brands in all categories under many different company names. It is safe to say that if a particular brand of liquor states that it is made or bottled by a company based in San Jose, it has been processed by Frank-Lin.

Owned by the Maestri family, the company is named after the parents, Frank and Lynn Maestri, with most of the day-to-day operations currently being handled by their three sons. The company holds copyrights on approximately 1,500 label names though they currently are marketing and distributing just eleven vodkas and seven gins, mainly in and around California.

The gin labels they represent are 'Barrett's', 'Bellringer 94.4°' an English import, 'Cossack', a label apparently under license, since it is also made by another company in the eastern U.S., 'Crown Russe' a label that is also made by Sazerac Inc., 'Glenwood', 'Martini 90°', and 'Potter's'.

In the vodka category they make, import or market and distribute 'Cardinal' vodkas, imported from the Netherlands and shared with Duggan's Distillers Products of New Jersey, 'Crown Czar', 'Crown Russe' (which is also made and marketed by Sazerac), 'Crown Superior', 'Cossack' (another shared label), 'Hertekamp' (imported from Belgium and shared with Duggans), 'Potter's' (under license), 'Real Light 50°', 'Royal Czar', 'Tamiroff', and 'White Wolf'.

They also modify, filter, and bottle the domestic premium vodka in the cobalt blue bottle 'Skyy', based in San Francisco.

Hood River Distillers

Located in Portland, Oregon, this small rectification company markets its products only in Oregon and Washington states. They manufacture and distribute four vodkas, 'Baron Rothschild', 'HRD', 'Monarch', and 'Three Star', plus a citron vodka under the 'Monarch' label. They also make and market two gins, 'Monarch' and 'Baron Rothschild'.

Heublein

While this company is now a part of the UDV/Diageo mega-conglomerate, it is interesting that the three vodkas they market are all produced in the standard manner. The neutral grain spirit is purchased from Grain Processing Co. and is modified to Heublein's specifications in a number of plants including those in Menlo Park, California, and in Hartford, Connecticut.

The fact that this company markets the #1, #2, and #16 best-selling vodka labels in the U.S. indicates that they must be doing something right. However, their labels are fluctuating with the overall market and all three labels have been showing declining sales figures in 1997, with Smirnoff going down 164,000 cases or 2.8 percent, Popov declining 228,000 cases or 8.1 percent, and Relska showing a decline of 54,000 cases or 14.6 percent. Overall the three brands showed a 1997 decline of 447,000 nine-liter cases from 1996, for a total sales decline of 4.90 percent.

Jim Beam Brands

This major supplier does make its own whiskeys in its Kentucky plant, but the two gins 'Calvert' and 'Gilbey's' and four vodkas 'Dark Eyes', 'Gilbey's', 'Wolfschmidt', and 'Kamchatka' that it represents are all standard production labels. The label 'Kamchatka' is shared with UDV/Diageo.

Laird and Company

This eighth-generation family-run company is the producer of 'Laird's Applejack' in their plant in New Jersey, but they also produce four gins, 'Banker's Club', 'Five O'clock', 'Laird's' and 'Senator's Club', plus five vodkas, with the same labels as listed plus 'Kasser's 51'. All are made in the standard manner with purchased spirit.

The Laird family first settled in Monmouth County, New Jersey, in 1698 when William Laird, an emigrant Scotsman came to this country. Once settled, he began production of Applejack for his own and his neighbors' consumption. One of his descendants, Robert Laird, left account books that show sales of Applejack as early as 1780, though the distribution and sale of the product certainly began sometime earlier. Prior to 1760, George Washington wrote to Robert Laird asking for his recipe for the production of Applejack. This company has an amazing history which moves right along with the history and growth of the United States. Today it is recognized as being the oldest operating distillery in the country, and is still managed by the eighth and ninth generations of the Laird family.

LeVecke Corporation

This Southern California (Mira Loma) firm manufactures and bottles for many other companies in the liquor and grocery business including Lucky Stores in California, but also has seven proprietary vodka labels: 'Danube', 'King's Deluxe', 'Sitka', 'Vanguard', 'Velvet Touch', 'Volska', and 'Volsky', plus a premium triple-distilled vodka in a distinctive bottle labeled 'Prism'. Their earnings for 1997 were $82 million which would place them on the major suppliers list.

Majestic Distilling Co.

This company based in Baltimore, Maryland, makes and markets eight vodkas, 'Bentley's', 'Black Watch', 'Classic Club', 'Lord Baltimore', 'Odesse', 'Rikaloff', 'Traveler's Club', and 'Zelko', all in the Mid-Atlantic area. They also make and market eight gins, with seven of the labels the same as above, the change being that there is no Zelko gin, and the other gin label is 'Club 400'.

McCormick Distilling Co.

The home offices of this company are located in Weston, Missouri, and they bottle and market one gin and one vodka, both labeled 'McCormick'. The company was originally the marketing and sales branch of Midwest

Grain Co., one of the Big Four grain-processing companies that distill high proof spirits in the grain belt.

A few years ago, the decision was made that Midwest
Grain should concentrate on its core business, so marketing and sales were spun off and sold to a couple of
employees. Midwest Grain still manufactures all of the
domestic products sold by this company, including the
gin which is a distilled gin, made in a gin head still at the
Midwest plant.

Montebello Brands Co.

Like Majestic, this rectifier is also based in Baltimore,
Maryland, and it makes and markets one gin, 'McColl's'
and three vodkas, 'McColl's', 'Vladimir', and 'Pride of
America'. There appears to be no connection between
the two Baltimore companies.

M.S. Walker Fine Wine & Spirits

Based in Somerville, Massachusetts, this company was
founded in 1929, as a purveyor of flavorings, syrups, and
extracts, but when Prohibition was repealed in 1934 they
began making alcoholic beverages. The company now
covers 70 percent of the U.S. with its products; it makes
and markets eight vodkas: 'Caldwell's', 'Cossack',
'Cossack Light', 'Lite 'n' Easy', 'Kimnoff', 'Kimnoff Light',
'Ruble', and 'S.S. Pierce', all in the standard manner.

Paramount Distillers Inc.

This rectifier is based in Cleveland, Ohio, and makes and
markets three vodkas, 'Paramount', 'Myer's', and 'Korski',
marketed in the Ohio river valley area. It makes no gins.

Phillips Products

Phillips Products is a Minneapolis company which
makes and markets the #17 best-selling vodka, 'Phillips',
with 1997 sales of 295,000 cases. They also own the
Millennium Import Co. which imports and markets two

of the Polish super-premium vodkas, Chopin and Belvedere.

Skyy Spirits

Skyy Spirits is actually a marketing company rather than a rectifier, but I felt they should be included here since they do market one of the fastest-growing of the vodkas. The company was founded by an entrepreneur named Maurice Kanbar, born and raised in New York City. He observed a need for an ultra-pure vodka when he kept getting hangovers after even a very small intake of alcohol, so he invented Skyy. The marketing, packaging, and product have all combined to make this one of the fastest-growing vodkas in the U.S. market. It's made from neutral spirit supplied by Frank-Lin of San Jose.

U.S. Distilled Products Co.

This company is based in St. Paul, Minnesota, and makes two gins labeled 'Hayes and Hunnicutt' and 'English Guard', both in the standard manner. They also import a Russian vodka labeled 'St. Petersburg' and make 'Karkov' vodka in the standard manner.

White Rock Distilleries

This rectifier and import company, located in Lewiston, Maine, makes and markets three labels of gins and vodkas. The brands are 'Gold Crown', 'Orloff, and 'Poland Spring', each of these names being applied to both a vodka and a gin.

White Rock is a family-run operation in which the Coulombe family are both owners and operators. The company is a full-range rectification company which both makes and imports products for sale in the upper New England area and distributes some products nationwide, one of which is the 'Aguila' brand of 100 percent *agave* añejo tequila.

American Vodka Importers

Importers play an outstanding role in the U.S. liquor industry. Most, though not all, imported vodkas are of the very finest quality, and currently U.S. vodka consumers are tending to switch to higher-priced imported vodkas.

Some of the rectifying companies listed above are also importers and may be represented here too. But for the most part this section deals with the companies whose primary business is the importation of fine-quality spirits, especially gins and vodkas.

A. Hardy USA

This Rosemount, Illinois, company is mainly known as the importer of A. Hardy cognacs, but it also imports, in concert with Mr. Elliott Rittenband, the vodka 'Original Polish', made by Polmos Bielsko-Biala.

A.I.G. Wine and Spirits

This small, dynamic New York company is importing the super-premium vodka 'Mezzaluna', and added a new super-premium gin, 'Kennsington', in 1999. The firm is owned and operated by Mr. Avery Goldberg.

Adamba Imports International Inc.

Owned by Mr. Adam Bak, this New York City–based company imports and distributes 'Luksosowa' potato vodka made by the Polmos Poznan distillery in Poland.

Carillon Importers

This company is now a part of UDV America/Diageo, and has been the importer of Stolichnaya Russian vodka for some time. They were the original importer of Absolut vodka from Sweden, prior to Seagram's America purchasing the U.S. distribution rights for that fine product. The company brought Stolichnaya into their portfolio at that time. One of the original salesmen for this company, Mr. Michel Roux, retired as president shortly after the merger and is now relaxing with a spirits company of his own.

Distillerie Stock USA

This company headquartered in Woodside, New York, is closely related to the Stock Company of Trieste, Italy. They import and market the vodka liqueurs from that company under the name of 'Keglevich'.

Domecq Importers

This company is now part of the Allied-Domecq company since it and the Hiram Walker liquor company were merged into one structure. Domecq imports the #2-selling British gin, 'Beefeater's', with 1997 sales of 640,000 nine-liter cases.

This company has grown through the years since its inception to become one of the largest players in the world. From the old Allied Distillers company of Great Britain to the merger with the Pedro Domecq wine and spirits company of Spain to being part of the fifth-largest selling liquor company in the U.S., Domecq has prospered through the years and looks to do so in the future.

Dozortsev and Sons, Ltd.

This New York City–based company is the importer and marketer of the 'Kremlovskaya' vodka line, with a plain vodka, a chocolate vodka, and a Limonnaya. The family-run operation was originally the U.S. importer and marketer for the vodka line based in Brussels, Belgium. In a meteoric climb, the vodka became the #2 best-selling vodka in the world. Then disaster struck, when the U.S.S.R. decided to triple the tax on imported vodka. Russia was the single largest customer that the company had, and so within a year the company was bankrupt.

The Dozortsev family purchased the company in Belgium and the rights to the name of the company. In order to start up in Russia again, they began making the vodka sold in Russia at the distillery in St. Petersburg. The vodkas sold in the rest of the world are manufactured in Belgium. The chocolate vodka is absolutely delicious.

Duggan's Distiller's Products

This Orangeburg, New Jersey, company used to import a Belgian vodka labeled 'Hertekamp', but dropped that brand from their portfolio in 1997. They are now importing a 'Cardinal' vodka made in Holland from sugar beets. It comes in both 80 and 90 proof versions.

Finnish National Distiller's

This company is the U.S. importer of Finlandia. Totally owned by the government of Finland, this company is the interface between the Finnish government and Brown-Forman, the national supplier of the brand.

Frank Pesce International Group Ltd.

This firm based in Boca Raton, Florida, is the importer of 'Cristall' vodka, which was originally one part of the Stolichnaya lineup of vodkas. Mr. Pesce now imports this vodka on an exclusive basis, and Cristall has been replaced in the Stolichnaya lineup by 'Stoli Gold'.

Hiram Walker & Sons

Now absorbed into the Allied-Domecq company, this company imported the #6 largest selling brand of vodka, 'Fris Skandia', made in Denmark, which sold 85,000 nine-liter cases in 1997.

Integrity Wine and Spirits

This rapidly-growing company is beginning to make its mark with two high-end super-premium products, 'French Alps' vodka and 'Citadelle' gin. Both are made in the Cognac region of France and show considerable originality. The owner is Mr. Mark Meisenhiemer of Los Angeles.

Joseph Seagram & Sons

This company is both a manufacturer and an importer, and imports 'Boodles' gin and the #1-selling imported vodka in the U.S., Absolut, with 1997 sales of 3,440,000 nine-liter cases. They also manufacture their own gin, Seagram's, the #1-selling gin in the US with 1997 sales of 3,170,000 nine-liter cases. They also had the only 'flavored' gin on the leading brands list, Seagram's Lime Twist, the #7 label with 1997 sales of 150,000 nine-liter cases. Their remaining products didn't make the leading brands list, but they also manufacture Seagram's Excel Gin.

Kettling Ridge Estate Wines and Spirits

Not strictly speaking an importer, this company is actually the Canadian concern supplying and possibly manufacturing Inferno vodka, the short, round, clear bottle with two red peppers visible in the vodka. They are experimenting with another version of this same idea, though one which uses tequila instead of vodka.

Millennium Import Co.

This Minneapolis company is the import arm of the Phillips Beverage Company of that same city and currently imports both Belvedere and Chopin vodkas from Poland.

Palm Bay Imports

This company is located in Syosset, New York, and is currently bringing in the #3-selling vodka worldwide, Wyborowa. They are also assembling a number of new brands for national distribution.

Pemar Importers

This very small company in Manhattan Beach, California, is currently bringing in the Russian vodka, 'Moskva Staraya', from the Kristall plant in Moscow. The company is owned and operated by Mr. Andy Patashnik.

Preiss Imports

Well-known for offering high-quality specialty items, this company operates from Southgate, California, in the Los Angeles basin. They import and market 'Van Hoo' vodka from the Fourcroy company in Holland and two gins, 'Horseguard' from Glasgow, Scotland, and 'Old Raj', made by the Springbank distillery in Campbeltown, Scotland.

Richmond Import Co.

This company imports and markets both gins and vodkas under the label name Black Death. It has 24 different flavors of vodkas, from Bubblegum to White Chocolate. While their marketing approach is different, these vodkas have won medals for the quality of their product in international competitions. Despite appearing as mere novelty items, these are serious vodkas of good quality. Based in Alamo in Northern California, Richmond Import is a wholly-owned subsidiary of the British company, Richmond Distillers.

Royal Kedem Wine Co.

Though this company's primary business is importing Israeli wines, they also import kosher vodkas from Israel. Two of them are 'Kedem" and 'Carmel'. The company is run by the Herzog family.

Sans Wine & Spirits

This company is based in Irvine, California, and is best known for importing products from Mexico and Central

America. They are currently importing from Mexico, a high-proof vodka made from rum, labeled 'Alcohol Victoria', and a somewhat lower-proof product from El Salvador, labeled 'Tic-Tac', the number one–selling vodka produced in El Salvador.

Schieffelin & Somerset

This New York City–based company is now a member of UDV/Diageo and imports the Tanqueray line of 'Tanqueray' and 'Tanqueray Malacca' gins, and the vodka labeled 'Tanqueray Sterling'.

Sidney Frank Importing Co.

Sidney Frank imports and markets the French super-premium vodka 'Grey Goose'. The company is based in New Rochelle, New York.

Todhunter International Co.

Based in West Palm Beach, Florida, this company is now importing 'Plymouth' gin after a 20-year absence. This product, made at the ancient Black Friars abbey in Plymouth, England, has returned and is again being accepted as the excellent product it has always been.

William Grant & Sons

Mainly known for its scotch whisky portfolio, William Grant also imports and markets the 'Grant's' gin label. This product no longer enjoys the status that it once did, but a resurgence in gin sales and the rebirth of the true martini may bring it back from its current obscurity. William Grant is headquarted in Edison, New Jersey.

SOME LEADING VODKAS COMPARED

Brand Name	Country of Origin	Raw Materials	Water Source	Distillation type	$ per 750
Absolut	Sweden	grain mixture	filtered well water	6-column still	15–20
Belvedere	Poland	purchased spirit	filtered wells	column still	25–30
Chopin	Poland	Stobrowa potatoes	Culligan water from deep well	column still	26–31
Finlandia	Finland	100 percent 6-row barley	glacial melt from arctic springs	7-column still	13–18
French Alps	France	special wheat from Brie	alpine spring water	pot still	20–25
Grey Goose	France	unknown	unknown	unknown	25–30
Ketel 1	Holland	purchased spirit from Germany and France	filtered Schiedam city water	column and redistill in copper pot still	15–20
Kremlovskaya	Belgium	unknown	unknown	column still	17–22
Krolewska	Poland	grain mixture	spring water	column still, 4 ×	20–25
Mezzaluna	Italy	unknown	unknown	column still	30–35
Original Polish	Poland	100 percent rye	filtered well water	column still	23–28
Rain	United States	organically grown corn	filtered water	column still	15–20
Skyy	United States	purchased spirit	filtered local water supply	column still	12–17
Smirnoff	United States	purchased spirit	filtered local water supply	column still	8–12
Stolichnaya	Russia	grain mixture	filtered river and lake water	column still	15–20
Sundsvall	Sweden	grain mixture	natural spring water	column still	30–35
Teton Glacier	United States	processed potatoes	filtered well water	column still	25–30

European Vodkas

Austria

This country makes at least one vodka which has been imported into the U.S. The J.A. Baczewski Co. in Vienna makes 'Vodka Monopolowa', a potato vodka imported by International Import Export Co. of Los Angeles.

Belarus

The largest and oldest of the current distilleries in this republic began operating in 1893. It is now called the Minsk Winery and Distillery (Minsk 'Kristall' W&D) which makes a new vodka now being imported into the U.S. The name of this vodka is 'Charodei'; the label is printed in the Cyrillic alphabet and packaged in a very nice 'cathedral window'–style frosted white bottle. The company has a long history and makes many different spirits, fortified wines, and liqueurs.

Belgium

One of the firms that produce vodkas in Belgium is the Fourcroy company which makes both the 'Iskra' and 'Van Hoo' labels. The latter is now imported into the U.S. by Preiss Imports, based in the Los Angeles area.

Another Belgian vodka is 'Hertekamp' which was at one time imported by Duggan's Distillers Products of New Jersey, but that company no longer imports this spirit.

Denmark

All of the distilleries in Denmark were combined into one company during 1989; it is now known as Danisco Distillers. All spirits currently made in Denmark are made by this company and distributed throughout Europe and the world. A few Danish vodkas from this company now for sale in the U.S. are 'Denaka', currently imported and marketed by Sazerac, 'Danzka', and 'Fris'. Fris is imported and marketed by Hiram Walker Inc.

El Salvador

This country produces a flavored sugarcane-derived spirit made from high proof alcohol. It is marketed under the name of 'Tic-Tac', and sells at 72 proof. It is the most popular spirit in El Salvador, and is currently being imported into the U.S. by Sans Wine & Spirits of Los Angeles

Estonia

This small Baltic country has at least one distillery that is now making and exporting vodka. The label 'Monopol' is made by the company A.S. Remedia in their distillery near the city of Kiiu. Liviko Distilleries in Tallinn produces two vodkas, 'Eesti Viin' and 'Viru Valge'.

Finland

The Primalco Company is the state-owned control agency for all spirits made in Finland. The primary products of this company are 'Finlandia' and 'Koskenkorva' vodkas which are exported throughout the world. 'Finlandia' is the major international export and 'Koskenkorva' is mainly sold in the areas of Europe geographically close to Finland. A new vodka developed to appeal to younger people is named 'Leningrad Cowboys', developed in association with the rock band of the same name.

France

Already celebrated for its many excellent alcoholic beverages, including wines and many of the finest brandies of the world, France now produces vodkas and gins. Two super-premium vodkas are imported into the U.S. from France: 'Grey Goose' vodka and 'French Alps', made at the Gabriel & Andreu cognac distillery which makes the 'Landy' brand of cognac, also near the town of Cognac. The distillery name and location of Grey Goose are supposed to be a proprietary 'mystery', though actually, according to my sources, it's made at the H. Mounier distillery in the town of Cognac, the maker of Polignac cognac. The vodkas '1822' and 'Ikanova' are made at the Boisset distillery in Nuits St. Georges but are not currently available in the U.S.

Great Britain

There are many companies in Britain that make vodkas and gins. (see Appendix F: the Gin and Vodka Association of Great Britain). Some of the vodkas imported into the U.S.A. are 'Black Death Vodka', made by Richmond Distilling Co. in 24 flavors, and The Original Black Vodka Co.'s 'Blavod'. (This is the only black vodka. Despite its name, Black Death doesn't produce a black vodka.) Other labels include 'Cossack', 'Smirnoff', 'Virgin', and 'Vladivar' (these all made in England), and 'Grant's', 'Karinskaya', and 'Sergei' (made in Scotland). However, the largest selling of the vodkas made in Great Britain is probably 'Tanqueray Sterling', made and marketed by United Distillers, now Diageo.

Iceland

This volcanic island produces at least two vodkas, 'Elduris', and 'Tindavodka', made by the Catco company in their Reykjavik bottling plant and 'Lord Dillon' gin from the same company. This company purchases the neutral grain spirit from distillers based on the island and then modifies it to the desired proof and condition by rectification and dilution with water from Icelandic springs.

Italy

Of the many distilleries in Italy, some do produce vodkas, both the flavored vodkas of the label 'Zone', made by Bonollo Umberto, and the 'Keglevich' vodka liqueur, which is made at the Stock Distillery in Trieste. A new super-premium vodka from Italy is 'Mezzaluna' vodka, a lightly lemoned spirit, made at the Distercoop distillery in Faenza and imported and marketed by A.I.G. Wines and Spirits of New York.

Latvia

The Lativjas Balzams Company in Riga makes many different types of spirits, and concentrates on liqueurs and closely associated types such as digestifs and aperitifs, but also make five vodkas, of which three are currently exported to the U.S. The U.S. import labels are 'Monopol', 'Rigalya', and 'Zelta'.

Netherlands (Holland)

Many spirit companies operate in the Netherlands, including the Nolet (Ketel 1 Vodka) and Dirkswager (Leyden Gin) distilleries in Schiedam, the Bols and De Kuyper groups of liqueur fame, Hooghoudt Distillers B.V. who make 'Royalty' vodka in their distillery near Groningen, plus many others. Almost all of them make vodkas and gins, including genevers. Since the Netherlands is the birthplace of gin, such is only to be expected. (For more information on the names and locations of the Dutch companies see Appendix C.)

Norway

The company Arcus Produkter, with four distilleries in the country, produces the potato vodka 'Vikingfjord' by buying in potato spirit from four other smaller distilleries and then rectifying it to 192 proof neutral spirit. The vodka is then diluted to bottle strength of 80 proof and 100 proof by adding melted water from glaciers which has had the calcium removed by an ion exchange system. They also produce 'Linie' aquavit.

Poland

This former vassal state of the U.S.S.R. has 25 distilleries inside the polmos conglomerate and one distillery privately owned by a joint venture of the Bols Co. of Holland and the Unicom company of Poland. One of the polmos distilleries is operating on an individual basis. Polmos Siedlce makes the super-premium vodka labeled

'Chopin' under its own direction and has exclusive rights to the name and and bottle design. Most other spirits manufactured by the polmoses are marketed on a worldwide basis by the Agros Trading Co. facility which handles the majority of sales of the spirits produced by the respective polmos facilities. But some of the polmoses are developing their own proprietary labels, such as 'Belvedere' made by Polmos Zyrardow.

There are reported to be over a thousand vodka labels manufactured and marketed in Poland, but they are forbidden to advertise inside Poland and many of them are now trying to come to the attention of the outside world. Some of the companies now importing Polish vodkas are Adamba Co. of New York City ('Luksusowa' potato vodka), Kensington House of Miami Beach ('Krowleska' vodka), A. Hardy & Co. outside Chicago ('Original Polish' vodka), Millennium Imports in Minneapolis ('Belvedere' and 'Chopin' vodkas), Palm Bay Imports of Syosset, New York ('Wyborowa' vodka) and Stanley Stawski Distilling Co., which imports more Polish vodkas than any other company in the U.S., with labels such as 'Harmas Jazz', 'Posejdon', 'Polmos', 'Polonaise', 'Premium', 'Zubrowka', 'Extra Zytnia', and 'C.K.'.

Of the 25 polmos distilleries in Poland, I have only been able to find eight that are exporting vodkas, including to the U.S. Those eight are located in the towns of Bielsko-Biala, Krakow, Lancut, Poznan, Siedlce, Starogard-Gdansk, Zielona-Gora, and Zyrardow. Agros Trading has been unable or unwilling to provide the names, addresses, or telephone numbers of the other polmoses who are supposedly producing vodka in Poland. I don't know why. Further research has enabled me to find the names of eight more of the polmoses: Polmos Gniezko, Polmos Jozefow, Polmos Lvov (now part of the Ukraine), Polmos Warsaw-Fuchs, Polmos Warsaw-Nowachowicz, Polmos Warsaw-Patsche, Polmos Warsaw-Rektifowany, and Polmos Wroclaw.

Russia

Sojuzplodoimport was formerly the state controlling agency for the spirits industry in the Soviet Union. Since the breakup of the Soviet Union, it has evolved into a marketing company jointly owned and controlled by the ten distilleries that are still making spirits in Russia. All of the companies have joint ownership of certain labels which can be made by any of the separate facilities. The most famous and the largest of the Russian distilleries is probably the Cristall facility in Moscow which makes 'Priviet', 'Staraya Moskva', 'Smirnoff Black Label', 'Stolichnaya Gold', 'Cristall' and others.

Many of these labels are imported into the U.S., the biggest-selling being 'Stolichnaya', which is imported and marketed by Carillon Imports (now part of Diageo). Stolichnaya encompasses two unflavored and ten flavored varieties of vodka. Others sometimes found in the U.S. are labels such as 'Moskovskaya Osobaya', 'Smirnoff Black Label', and 'Ultraa' which was imported for a couple of years by a Florida company. Of the ten distilleries which form the Sojuzplodoimport group, only seven appear to be of importance. These distilleries are located in the cities of Irkutsk, Kaluga, Kaliningrad, Kursk, Moscow, Samara, and St. Petersburg. I was unable to get the names of the remaining three distilleries or of the cities where they are located.

The St. Petersburg distillery also makes and exports a vodka labeled 'St. Petersburg', imported and marketed by the United States Distilled Products Co. of St. Paul , Minnesota.

Spain

Rives Pitman S.A., a subsidiary of the giant Osborne brandy producer located in the town of Puerto de Santa Maria, distills and markets the vodka label 'Von Haupold' at its distillery in that town. This company is also the largest producer of gin in Spain and uses a triple distillation process through continuous action column stills to produce a high-quality neutral grain spirit.

Sweden

'Absolut' vodka is one of the primary exports of the V. & S. Vin and Spirits Co. a monopoly of the wholly-owned government-controlled spirits industry of Sweden. A new super-premium vodka labeled 'Sundsvall' was introduced into the U.S. in September of 1998. The company stresses that this vodka is not made by Absolut, but both are owned by V. & S. Vin and Spirits and marketed in the U.S. by Joseph E. Seagram and Sons.

Another Swedish vodka currently available in the U.S. is labeled 'Svedka', imported by Spirits Marque One, of Dallas, Texas.

Ukraine

This country has at least one distillery which is exporting vodka to the U.S., the Artyomovsk distillery in the city of Donetsk. The vodka it exports is called 'Old Kiev'.

Vodkas from the Rest of the World

El Salvador

'Tic-Tac' is the most popular spirit in El Salvador, and is exported at a strength of 72 proof. This would make it a cordial or light vodka under BATF regulations, but it is rectified from high-proof spirits and is simply a slightly dilute vodka product.

Korea

Manufactured in Seoul from rice alcohol, 'Jinro' is classified as a 'soju' or 'shochu'. Jinro is probably the world's biggest-selling vodka-type drink (it certainly was a few years ago). It actually qualifies as a cordial or liqueur, being only 48 proof (24 percent alcohol), and having some sugar and citric flavoring added. Though sometimes hard to find, it is available in the U.S.

Mexico

A high (99) proof sugarcane-derived spirit named 'Alcohol Victoria' is now being imported into the U.S. and marketed by Sans Wine and Spirits Co., Los Angeles.

The importer originally stated he didn't think that this product qualified as a vodka, but later changed his mind. It's distilled in a column still to over 190 proof before being processed and bottled. The only question about this spirit's claim to be a vodka is whether it has gone through charcoal filtration.

Puerto Rico

'Exclusiv' is a drink made at the Bacardi facility in Puerto Rico, and is normally included in the U.S.-made products category.

St. Kitts

'Cane Spirit Rothschild' is made from sugarcane juice on the Caribbean island of St. Kitts. This drink is often thought of as a rum, but as it is distilled out at 191 proof, it is really a vodka. The company was founded by Baron Edmund Rothschild of the famous wine family. Unfortunately the baron passed away in 1997, and the distillery is currently not operating. Cane Spirit Rothschild is still available in Caribbean locations, and is reported to be very clean with few congeners—a true sugarcane vodka.

4

The Expanding Universe of Flavored Vodkas

Age cannot wither her, nor custom stale
Her infinite variety.

William Shakespeare, *Antony and Cleopatra*

Vodka is the universal liquor. Its enormous appeal springs largely from its versatility: you can be sure that vodka will mix with anything. So vodka has historically taken a path diametrically opposed to that of all other drinks: whereas they all try to retain special distinguishing charactersitics, vodka tries to eliminate these, making the absence of such characteristics vodka's own special characteristic: 'purity' or 'clarity'.

Having achieved something that will mix with anything, the next step is to mix it. So why not do the mixing at the factory, and provide consumers with a ready-mixed drink?

The pioneer of the flavored vodkas was gin. Gin began as something very different from its modern form, but it always depended upon the addition of flavoring agents after the completion of the distillation process—though in the beginning, these flavoring agents were valued chiefly for their medicinal properties. As gin changed over time, it gradually became a flavored vodka. You can, of course, make your own gin, simply by steeping juniper berries and other herbs and spices in vodka.

The universe of flavored vodkas is a fast-changing universe, a cosmos in turmoil. And it is rapidly expanding: more flavored vodkas are appearing all the time. Here I can only give a hint of this exciting area.

Are flavored vodkas the wave of the future in alcoholic drinks? A century from now, will most people think of a liquor as alcohol and water with flavor added subsequent to distillation? Or is this a gimmicky, ephemeral craze, destined to die away like so many other novelties? Only time will tell.

The Schnappses

Among flavored vodkas, we must also consider flavored schnappses, aquavits, and (further flavored!) gins. Schnapps is a slightly different version of vodka, since it normally is allowed to keep some of the congeners that are removed when making a vodka. But the product schnapps is not so different that its character will interfere with whatever flavors the manufacturer may add to the base spirit.

One of the main differences between the flavored schnappses and the other flavored vodkas is that the regular vodkas will normally be flavored with natural fruit essences, while schnappses may use any flavoring that can be found, including many that are artificial. There are many examples of flavored schnapps products on the market, ranging from butterscotch to cinnamon, menthol to chocolate, and including many of the generic flavors of the standard liqueurs. Most of the flavored schnappses are classified as cordials by the BATF, since they are sweetened, and bottled and marketed at less than 80 proof. According to the federal regulations, any product that is less that 80 proof or has more than 2.5

percent sugar must legally be classified as a cordial or a liqueur.

But the same is true of many of the acknowledged 'flavored vodkas'. Many of Stolichnaya's flavored vodkas are only 70 proof, which places them under the limit and makes them liqueurs under federal regulations. 'Stoli' has ten flavored plus three unflavored variants, and eight of these products fall into the classification of a cordial, with only two of the flavored variants being 80 proof or more, the Limonnaya at 80 proof and the Okhotnichya at 90 proof.

There is another product line of vodkas that is even more extensive than the Stolis, however, and that is the hugely successful British line of 'Black Death' vodkas with 24 flavors, plus the unflavored variant. The line consists of flavors that also have the names of Russian cities associated with them. The flavors are: aniseed (Kirov), banana (Buysk), blackjack (Tomsk), bubblegum (Minsk), cherry (Samara), chili pepper (St. Petersburg), chocolate (Omsk), cinnamon (Novosibirsk), coffee (Penza), garlic (Chita), ginger (Tobolsk), lemon (Kyzil), lime (Murmansk), orange (Vobonelh), peach (Serov), peardrop (Nizhny Tagil), peppermint (Kemerove), raspberry (Norilsk), sherbet (Yakutsk), strawberry (Arkhangelsk), throat lozenges (Orel), tropical (Bodaybo), vanilla (Kotuy), and white chocolate (Nizhny Novghorod). Though highly popular in Europe, most of these flavors are not currently available in the U.S., but the unflavored version can occasionally be found. (Incidentally, though the firm is called 'Black Death', it does not make black vodka: only Blavod, a different British company, does that.)

There are innumerable schnappses of myriad types and qualities. One of the premium schnappses being sold in the U.S. is labeled 'Goldschlager', a 100 proof cinnamon-flavored product with tiny flakes of gold leaf floating in the liquid. Then there are the mint schnappses, menthol, and all the flavors of the taste spectrum, all of the citrus styles, from orange to tangerine, coffee, chocolate, and many others. I have yet to see a kiwi flavor, but I'm sure I won't have long to wait.

The Aquavits

Aquavits, akavits, or akvavits are products of the countries around the Baltic. These drinks are vodkas that have been flavored with caraway seeds, giving them a nose and flavor reminiscent of New York rye bread and closely resembling 'Kümmel', a flavored schnapps product from Germany. Since almost all of them are made in the different countries around the Baltic Sea, and all of these countries speak different languages, the spelling of the word differs from country to country and brand to brand.

Some of the labels do use additional flavors in their aquavits however, at least one, 'Riemersholms Herrgard', adds a touch of whiskey and ages the spirit in used sherry barrels after the product is distilled in Sweden. 'Linie' is made at the Arcus distillery in Oslo, Norway, and some of their American representatives claim that the product is produced using only caraway seed as the grain that is fermented. This seems incredible, but since I haven't yet been able to talk to anyone from the home office in Oslo, I can't unequivocally say that the statement is wrong. The third company which makes akvavit available in the U.S. is Danisco, the producer of Aalborg akvavit in Denmark, plus their akvavit liqueur 'Jubileaum'. Many other aquavits produced in some of the Baltic states are completely unavailable in the U.S..

Comparing flavored vodkas and flavored schnappses, the vodkas will usually be higher in alcohol proof levels and lower in sugar. This is not always true, as some of the flavored schnapps products may run as high as 100 proof and some of the imported vodka liqueurs are as low as 40 proof.

A large portion of the growth trend in vodkas is coming from the flavored segment. Gins are also experimenting with flavored versions (in addition to the usual gin botanicals, of course), notably 'Seagram's Lime Twist'. Sales of that brand has grown from zero in 1995 to 150,000 cases in 1997.

From Covering Up the Bad to Enhancing the Good

Flavored beverages do appear to be an indicator of the immediate future of the vodka or clear spirits market. Traditionally, flavored vodkas always were a significant part of the total vodka market, but in the past the flavors were mainly used to conceal bad tastes that were left in the vodka because of the inferior distillation processes of a bygone era. A great deal can be covered up if you add enough herbs, honey, sweeteners and other flavors to your product. With some of the flavored vodkas from antiquity containing more than a score of different herbs or flavors (such as Gnesnania Boonekamp, a bitters style vodka), it becomes clear that the current trend of flavors is a rebirth of the old ways, though for rather different reasons. But survivors of bygone ages may feed into the new trend. Many ancient techniques of food preparation, like pickles and curries, were invented to cover bad tastes and preserve the food in the days before refrigeration, but are now accepted for purely esthetic, gustatory reasons.

Some of the ancient styles of flavored vodkas still being made today, and in some cases imported into the U.S., include obscure flavored vodkas, like 'Tarkhuna', flavored with an herb from the broad steppes of what used to be part of Russia, now the independent country of Georgia, and 'Zubrovka', the famous bison-grass vodka. The new manufacturing standards do not allow the traditional method of placing a blade of this grass in the bottle as in times past however. Now they must use the essence or oils from the grass to flavor the finished product. Some health-related requirement, I am given to understand; the powers that regulate such things evidently think that the consumer will choke on the grass and suffer grave and serious injuries. Sometimes I wish bureaucrats could use just a little common sense.

Then there are many other flavored vodkas from all over the world, like the Chinese vodka 'Great Wall' which uses sesame seeds; 'Jinro', the Korean 48-proof sweetened citrus vodka; and many others that haven't yet come to the attention of American importers.

While the older flavorings were used to cover up bad tastes, the two main reasons for the new styles of flavorings are to create more variety and to make the bartender's life easier. Many bartenders or mixologists use the flavored varieties of vodka to speed up their preparation of certain types of mixed drinks. Just as they sometimes invent or re-invent drinks to use up out-of-date liquor stock and then run specials on these cocktails until the product is gone.

Almost every week, there is a new label or variant of the flavored vodkas presented to the marketplace. In 1998, an almost original gimmick vodka labeled 'Inferno' came on the market. Imported from Canada and flavored by placing two red peppers inside the bottle containing the vodka, the pepper flavor is gradually infused into the vodka over time and slowly changes its color and taste. The longer it sits, the redder the vodka gets. It finally becomes a reddish-brown color. I was told that it tastes like tequila, but I didn't believe this for a moment, since tequila doesn't taste anything at all like peppers. And sure enough, when I did taste Inferno I found that I'd been right.

There are other products that call themselves flavored vodkas or even vodka liqueurs. Immediately the labels 'Zone' and 'Keglevich' come to mind. Both are very smooth and light, simply because they are of a relatively low proofage. Keglevich is only 20 percent alcohol or 40 proof and Zone is 25 percent alcohol or 50 proof. Both use only natural flavors and are very fine and luscious to the palate.

It might be wise to be very careful when drinking either of these products since they go down so smoothly and taste so wonderful that the alcohol content can sneak up on you quite unobtrusively. Both are stronger than a mixed drink, but are very good straight and could be mixed with plain club soda for a nice fruit spritzer. However the sweetness of either of these products could make for a very unpleasant hangover the next day. Both products are made in Italy.

The other flavored variants of vodka are everywhere, but another of the new flavors that seems poised to take off is the 'Kremlovskaya' Belgian chocolate vodka. It's truly different from all others that I have tried, it appears to be of the highest quality and tastes wonderful. There are a number of cocktails which use this new vodka; one of the best is called the 'Chocolate Kiss'.

Any and all of these flavors can be and are used in preparing mixed drinks by bartenders and many new recipes are available that use them. Mixologists will normally use them to save time when preparing a cocktail that calls for certain ingredients. Use of a Limonnaya, for example, when the recipe calls for vodka and lemon juice. Each of the other available flavors were designed with other drinks in mind.

By the way, the difference between a bartender and a mixologist can be confusing, but normally a bartender serves the patrons at a sit-down style bar, where a mixologist would usually work a very busy service-style bar. The bartender is more of a people type of guy and a mixologist has acquired the facility for making drinks very fast.

New flavors are constantly being developed and marketed and will certainly continue to be so developed. As long as the flavored portion of the vodka market continues to grow at the current pace, new products will continue to be introduced. Entrepreneurs, companies, and customers keep on trying new things until something clicks and becomes a success.

Making Your Own Flavored Vodkas

It's quite easy to make your own flavored vodkas. While the prices of the flavored variants of the different labels are almost always the same price as the unflavored product, it can be fun to see if you can make a better flavor than the vodka companies themselves.

It's very simple to obtain the botanicals used to make a gin product of your own. Most can be found in any spice or herb store, and oil of juniper should be obtainable through a bakery or specialized herb supply store. You can find many different flavors in your local grocery store. An Italian company, Torani, makes many different flavoring syrups which could also be used to make flavored vodkas. Though these flavors are normally used to make sno-cones, they will serve to flavor many other products, vodka included.

Then there are the many recipes floating around on how to make your own 'sloe gin', plus recipes for kahlúa or coffee-flavored vodka, using vodka, instant coffee, vanilla bean, and sugar. Some people believe that the rectification companies will eventually make all of their alcoholic beverages this way, just by adding flavorings. For bourbon, just add a bourbon flavoring, for brandy, add brandy flavoring, and so on. Professionals in the industry sometimes boast that most plants are run by computers and can make any type of alcoholic beverage from flavorings and neutral grain spirits. If this were true, then eventually all liquors could become in reality flavored vodkas.

But we're a long way from that outcome being practically feasible, at least for the best-quality whiskeys, brandies, rums, or tequilas, and in any case there is a legal obstacle. Most classifications of spirits are determined by the basic raw materials from which they are made. It's unlawful to make a product from a vodka or a neutral grain spirit, and then sell it as 'brandy', 'whiskey', or 'tequila'. Brandy, for instance, has to be distilled from the fermented juice of fruits, either tree or vine, and the neutral grain spirit used by most rectification plants does not fulfill that criteria.

The same holds true of rums, which must be made from molasses or the juice of the sugar cane plant, and many other classifications. The main difference between the neutral grain spirit and whiskey is time, however. Whiskey must always be stored in oak for a few years; normally three to five years is the minimum, though the starting place for vodka and whiskey is the same, neutral grain spirits. As a matter of fact, the primary ingredient for the blended scotch category is neutral grain spirits, which then has the single malts added as the flavoring agents to turn it into scotch. It is then aged for the required time. But here, of course, the 'flavoring' is itself a distilled spirit.

One of the easiest types of liqueurs to make is the anise-flavored spirits of the European continent. The flavors of anisette or ouzo (even sambuca and campari use this haunting flavor) can be achieved by simply soaking various types of herbs or berries in spirits until the spirit takes on the flavor of the herbs, spices, or fruits through the mixing of the spirit and the juices of the fruit in an infusion which makes the two flavors one. To facilitate the mixing, the bottle containing the spirit should be rotated once a day.

This is the basic recipe for that most misunderstood beverage of my youth, 'sloe gin', which can be made by the infusion of sloe berries into a portion of gin. If you take a one-quart mason jar, pack it full of ripe sloe berries and fill the jar with gin, seal it and leave it in a cool dark place for one or more months, when you take it down you will have a bottle of sloe gin.

When I was a youth in high school, it seems that every male teenager of high school age managed to come up with a bottle of sloe gin when he was out with his buddies on a weekend night. I don't really know why this was so; perhaps it was only in Texas and Oklahoma that this phenomenon occurred. But when I was growing up, it seemed that sloe gin was the one spirit that high school kids could get their hands on. I don't think I ever tasted it, for I have no recollection of its flavor.

There are many other ways to flavor alcohol. The cordials and liqueurs started in the same way, by trying different natural flavors to flavor vodkas and gins. Of course we know where the botanicals that flavor gin come from—with very few exceptions, right out of your own kitchen spice cabinet. And the flavors of the vodkas come from many of the native fruits, herbs, and even grasses that grow in the areas where vodka originated, like the bison grass used to flavor Zubrowka, or the tarragon used to flavor 'Tarkhuna', from the steppes of Georgia, or the 'Tatra Vodka', from the highlands of Southern Poland. All of these plus many others show the way of the flavored vodkas.

There have been many other types of flavored vodkas, from the bitters-style 'Gnesnania Boonekamp' Polish vodka, which is flavored with 23 different herbs and spices and said to be an excellent 'digestive' tonic to cure many aliments, to 'Krupnik', a honey- and spice-flavored vodka which was employed as a medication, with at least one Prince of Poland (actually Prince Gedymin of Lithuania) claiming that it had cured him of a deadly disease.

The Russians make a highly flavored and spiced vodka labeled 'Okhotnichaya', which has port wine, infusions of ginger and turmentil roots, angelica, cloves, black and red pepper, juniper berries, coffee, star anise seeds, plus orange and lemon peel. To read the recipe puts you in mind of a strangely flavored strong gin, but it has been popular in Russia for many years and is imported and distributed in the U.S. as one of the Stolichnaya flavored vodkas.

Other flavors that can be used to modify vodka are beyond the limits of most people's imaginations. The list composed by the Black Death brand of vodka with their 24 labels is only the beginning of the story. In the old days there was a Polish vodka in which an adder was immersed for a period of weeks or even months. It was called 'Zmijowka'. I have seen a novelty bottle of spirit from southeast Asia in which a small cobra was immersed. Interesting to look at. I can't say what it tastes like. But I know that we will see stranger things in the years ahead.

5
Vodka Tasting Notes

There on a little table was a tray, laid with slices of white bread and butter, pressed caviar in a glass bowl, pickled mushrooms on a saucer, something in a little saucepan, and finally, vodka in one of the jeweller's ornate decanters The decanter was so chilled that it was wet with condensation from standing in a finger-bowl full of cracked ice.

Mikhail Bulgakov, *The Master and Margarita*

This chapter provides tasting notes for most of the leading vodkas or vodka-related drinks, in the following order: American vodkas, Western European vodkas, Polish vodkas, Russian-style (Russian, Ukrainian, and Belorussian) vodkas, vodkas from the rest of the world, aquavits, flavored vodkas, and vodka liqueurs.

Accurate tasting is not something we do naturally, but it is a skill which can be learned by anyone. It is the art of objective observation, yet it always keeps a personal element. You should trust your own nose and palate against the opinions of 'experts', but if you are new to this art, the following notes will help you to know what you're looking for. For advice on how to conduct a tasting, and how to taste, see Chapter 11.

American Vodkas

Barton's Charcoal Filtered Vodka, 80 proof

Clean and bright with no color and good legs. The nose is flinty with a light undertone of di-acetyl ketone and a medium nasal burn; a light fruit nose was observed on the next sniff. In the mouth the first sip is sweetish with almost no burn and few other discernible flavors. The aftertaste is dry and long with a light tinge of fruit.

Crater Lake Vodka, 80 proof

Clear and clean with no color and long slender legs. Very light aromas of any kind, and no nasal burn. In the mouth there is almost no flavor of any kind, a little sweetish, and no burn. The aftertaste has a sweetish slate flavor with a long finish.

Crystal Palace Vodka, 80 proof

Clear and clean with no color and long legs. To the nose there is a slight caramel aroma with little nasal burn. In the mouth there is a light caramel sweetness with no burn and little oiliness. The aftertaste does show a little burn down the throat and is lightly sweet with a long finish.

Dark Eyes Vodka, 80 proof

Clean with a hint of brown and broken legs. The nose shows light caramel with a medium nasal burn and a hint of acetone. In the mouth there is a slight taste of caramel sweetness, little burn, and the liquid is slightly chewy. The aftertaste is even sweeter and cloying, with a long finish.

Everclear Vodka, 84 proof

Clear and clean with no color and long, slender legs. A light acetone nose with a medium nasal burn. Oily in the mouth with some chewiness and an inherent sweetness and light burn to the center of the tongue. The aftertaste reveals an even sweeter flash and a continued burn which slowly ebbs to a long finish.

Fleischmann's Vodka, 80 proof

Clean with a light hint of brown and long medium thick legs. To the nose it shows a null aroma with a light nasal burn. In the mouth there is a crisp tartness at first which evolves to a strong burn to the entire interior of the mouth; the vodka is lightly oily and has a very light chewiness. The aftertaste shows a sweet caramelly flavor with a long finish.

Gilbey's Vodka, 80 proof

Clean with a hint of gray and long wide legs. The nose shows a feel of acetone and caramel, with light nasal burn. In the mouth there is a slight astringency which leads to a clean sweetness and light mouth burn. The aftertaste is sweet with a long finish and no burn.

Glenmore Vodka, 80 proof

Clean and bright with no color and long slender legs. the nose is dry and biting with no off aromas and a light nasal burn. In the mouth there is a charcoal astringency which fades to sweetness and a medium burn in the front of the mouth. Slightly oily and some chewiness. The aftertaste is sweet and caramelly with a long finish and some burn.

Gordon's Vodka, 80 proof

Clean, clear, and bright, with long slender legs. To the nose there is a hint of caramel with a light nasal burn. In the mouth there is light charcoal and some sweetness, with little oiliness, no chewiness and little burn. The aftertaste is sweet and shows a slight burn which changes to a throaty burn and a long finish.

Iceberg Vodka, 80 proof

Clean, clear, and bright, with no color and long, medium-width legs. To the nose there is almost no aroma at all, with little nasal burn. In the mouth, the vodka is very soft with a little sweetness and light mouth burn. The aftertaste is lightly sweet and a little unsettling to my stomach, with a long finish.

Jacquin's Royale Vodka, 80 proof

Clear and clean with a light touch of beige and long wide legs. To the nose it is caramelly with a lemon zest overtone and a light nasal burn. In the mouth it is sweet with a medium burn and a light oiliness with almost no other flavors. The aftertaste is sweet with a light throat burn and a medium finish.

Kamchatka Vodka, 80 proof

Clear and clean with no color and broken legs. To the nose it has an acetone feel with a medium nasal burn and a very light off tone like dirty clothes. In the mouth there is a certain sweetness with a medium burn and few other flavors. The aftertaste has a sweet oily feel with a light tang of something I can't identify and a medium finish.

Laird's Vodka, 80 proof

Clear and clean with no color and broken legs. To the nose there is a light toffee overtone with almost no nasal burn. In the mouth there is a certain sweetness with a medium burn to the lips and tongue. The aftertaste is light and clean with a medium finish.

Mr. Boston Vodka, 80 proof

Clear and clean, with no color and long medium legs. To the nose there is acetone combined with a light caramel overtone and a light nasal burn. In the mouth there is a light acidic feel with some sweetness and a medium burn to the tongue. The aftertaste is medium alcohol with some sweetness and a medium finish.

Nikolai Vodka, 80 proof

Clean and bright, with no color and long, medium legs. In the nose is a lemon overtone with a strong nasal burn. In the mouth there is a light sweetness and some oiliness with few flavors other than alcohol and a light burn. The aftertaste is lightly sweet with a long finish.

Popov Vodka, 80 proof

Clean and clear, with a light tint of gray and long medium legs. In the nose there is some acetone and a hint of caramel with little nasal burn. In the mouth there is a charcoal flintiness with a level sweetness and some burn. The aftertaste reveals a throat burn and an even stronger sweetness with a long sweet finish.

Rain Vodka, 80 proof

Clear and clean, with a hint of beige and long, slender legs. To the nose there is a hint of a fruity aroma with a light nasal burn. In the mouth there is a light feel, no oiliness and a hint of sweetness with little burn. The aftertaste shows some warmth with a sweet long finish.

Riva Vodka, 80 proof

Clean and bright, with no color and long slender legs. To the nose there is a light acetone with a medium nasal burn and a hint of vegetation. In the mouth there is a warmth that grows and little other flavor except alcohol, with a medium burn. The aftertaste shows some sweetness and a little cloying taste with a long finish.

Schenley Vodka, 80 proof

Clear and clean with just a hint of straw color and long, medium-width legs. To the nose there is a light hint of acetone combined with a citrus overtone and a medium nasal burn. In the mouth there is a little flint probably from charcoal, some sweetness, and a medium burn to the tongue. The aftertaste shows mainly alcohol with an inherent sweetness a little throat burn and a long sweet finish.

Skol Vodka, 80 proof

Clean and bright, with no color and long slender legs. A light di-acetyl aroma with alcohol and a medium nasal burn. In the mouth there is a crisp beginning which moves to a strong burn to the tongue. The aftertaste shows sweetness with a medium throat burn and a long finish.

Skyy Vodka, 80 proof

Clear, clean, and bright, with no color and long, slender legs. The nose reveals only alcohol with a light nasal burn and no off tones. In the mouth there is a neutral taste with a light sweetness, a hint of charcoal and a medium burn to the center of the tongue. The aftertaste reveals more sweetness with a neutral flint and a long finish. This is just about the purest-tasting vodka I've ever sampled. It's extraordinarily clean, with fewer obtrusive flavoring elements than any of the other offerings.

Smirnoff Vodka Red Label, 80 proof

Clean and clear, with a hint of straw color and medium broken legs. To the nose there is light acetone and a strong nasal burn. In the mouth there is a beginning dryness with a good burn to the center of the tongue and a very slight sweetness. The aftertaste reveals a mild sweetness, neutral flavors, and a medium finish.

Smirnoff Vodka Blue Label, 100 proof

Clear and clean, with no color and long slender legs. To the nose there are few aromas except alcohol with a medium nasal burn. In the mouth there is an immediate burn to the tongue, some flint or charcoal, and a certain oiliness with no chewiness. The aftertaste is lightly harsh with a strong throat burn, a little lemony tang, and a long finish.

Taaka Vodka, 80 proof

Clean and clear, with a light tinge of brown with long broken legs. The nose shows a good orange aroma with a slight acetone feel and a light alcohol nasal burn. In the mouth there is a neutral sweetness with a medium burn to the tongue and no oiliness. The aftertaste is tingly with a medium throat burn, some sweetness, and a long finish.

Taaka Platinum Vodka, 80 proof

Clean and clear, with a light beige feel and long, medium legs. To the nose there is a metallic overtone with a light astringency, possibly a light citrus overtone and little nasal burn. In the mouth there is a very light citrus feel with a medium burn to the roof of the mouth and few other flavors. The aftertaste shows a stronger lemon flavor and a medium sweetness with a long finish.

Teton Glacier Potato Vodka, 80 proof

Clean and bright, with no color and fast-moving long, slender legs. To the nose there is no aroma at all except for alcohol and a light nasal burn. In the mouth there is a light sweetness, no oiliness, a medium burn to the center of the tongue and no other flavors. The aftertaste reveals a medium sweetness and a clean palate with a light throat burn and a good long finish. This vodka is a real find: silky smooth and goes down clean and neat.

Tito's Handmade Vodka, 80 proof

Clear and clean, with a very light hint of gray and with long, very light legs. To the nose there is a hint of vegetable mustiness, akin to cauliflower, and a slight metallic overtone with a medium nasal burn. In the mouth, a cool beginning warms to a light burn to the tongue, a slight sweetness and a hint of a bean feel with no oiliness. The aftertaste reveals even more sweetness, a medium throat burn, and a long, sweet finish. A vodka to look out for.

Wolfschmidt Vodka, 80 proof

Clean and clear, with a hint of gray and long, slender legs that break at the bottom. To the nose there is a very light caramel aroma with some acetone and a light nasal burn. In the mouth there is an immediate sweetness with a light charcoal taste and a light burn to the tongue. The aftertaste is sweet and cloying, with a long, sweet finish.

Western European Vodkas

Absolut Vodka, 80 proof (Sweden)

Clear and clean, with a slight grayish tint, good viscosity with long legs and smooth slippage down the side of the glass. To the nose there is a slight meaty aroma, plus some alcohol burn to the sinuses and a very light aroma of acetone. In the mouth, the first sip comes with a sweetish grain taste but very little burn anywhere and no attack at all, just a slight tingle to the front part of the tongue. The finish is fairly long with a neutral aftertaste which grows slightly sweeter and dies away. The mouth feel is almost chewy. With the addition of a little water, the meaty nose becomes more pronounced and the taste is a little bitter.

Blavod's Original Black Vodka, 80 proof (United Kingdom)

The solid black color appears to be in suspension within the liquid and does not streak the glass at all. At the edge of the liquid inside the glass it gradually becomes slightly lighter until there is a bluish to clear edge where it meets the glass. Good legs and only the clear vodka slides down the glass; there is no color to the legs. Otherwise the liquid looks as black as ink. To the nose there is a slight citrus feel with no alcohol burn and no readily discernible off aromas. In the mouth there is a little heat to the edges and tip of the tongue with some sting in the center, a slight sweetness to combat the burn. The aftertaste reveals a smooth sweetness with a very light heat to the back of the mouth and no burn in the throat with a long finish. Don't dismiss this vodka because of its novelty appearance; it's a fine-quality drink, comparable in flavor to many more expensive and un-novel vodkas.

Cardinal Vodka, 80 proof (The Netherlands)

In a wasp-waisted frosted white bottle, the vodka appears clear and clean with long slender legs. The nose reveals a clean citric aroma with little burn and a suggestion of toffee. In the mouth it is clean with little burn, a smooth light sweetness and just a hint of subtlety. The aftertaste is neutral and almost non-existent with an easy, long finish. This is the only vodka I have experienced which is made from sugar beets.

Cardinal Vodka, 90 proof (The Netherlands)

In a black wasp-waisted bottle, the vodka appears clear and clean with even more slender long legs. To the nose, the vodka has even less character than Cardinal's 80-proof version, with no nasal burn and just a hint of alcohol. In the mouth, there is a metallic taste that is not unpleasant but has a light astringency and the feel of smoothness with no burn, lightly chewy with very little aftertaste and a long finish.

Denaka Vodka, 80 proof (Denmark)

Clean and bright with very long legs and light viscosity. The first nose has a citrus feel with light alcohol and no nasal burn, while later sniffs show more alcohol and a lemon cake aroma. The first sip has a sweet lemon curd taste with a little alcohol burn concentrated in the center of the tongue and at the back of the throat on swallowing. The finish is long and sweetish with a lingering burn to the tongue which slowly ebbs away to a clean slightly sweet end.

Doornkaat (Germany)

Very pale yellowish tinge, good viscosity with long legs and slight chatoyance. Grainy nose with caramel and cooked meat aromas and a medium alcohol burn to the sinus. First sip has a sweetish burn to the center of the tongue, with a tingle to the back of the throat and a different aftertaste. The aftertaste is sweet and lingering, with a mellow burn that dies slowly to a neutral finish.

Finlandia Vodka, 80 proof (Finland)

Very clean and bright in clarity, with good viscosity, long legs and good drainage down the side of the glass. To the nose, very little aroma, except a very light alcohol sinus burn. The second nosing reveals nothing added to the aroma. In the mouth there is a slight tingle in the front which slowly grows stronger until it peaks with a glowing heat throughout the mouth. The balance is good, and a slight sweetness makes itself evident at the finish with a long glide to a sweetly grainy end. Smooth and clean overall with a good mouth feel and crisp burn down the throat. The meticulous attention to detail in manufacturing and choice of raw materials comes through in the final product. Finlandia is one of the finest of the 'Western vodkas' and decidely superior to some that cost twice as much.

French Alps, 80 proof (France)

Above-average viscosity, good sheeting action, and long legs. Clean and clear with a pale yellow straw tinge and light chatoyance. Light toffee nose with no alcohol burn to the nasal passages. Sweet, slightly chewy first sip with light alcohol burn to the center of the tongue and almost no aftertaste or attack of any kind. Some sweetness at the finish with a mellow feel to the throat.

Fris Vodka Skandia, 80 proof (Denmark)

Clean and bright with good viscosity, long legs, and some color refraction. A slight burn to the nasal cavities is evident at first nosing, but the overall feel is clean and pleasant with a very light caramel feel rather than an actual aroma. The first sip reveals a clean, sweet taste which tingles the tongue very lightly and increases to a light burn. There is little chewiness and the second sip reveals a little more heat to the center of the tongue. The finish is long with the sweetness continuing to the end and slowly ebbing to a silent sigh.

Fuerst Bismarck (Germany)

Good viscosity, smooth sheeting action and long legs, with a slight greyish tinge. Very little aroma of any kind, with no alcohol burn to the nasal passages. Light alcohol feel to the center of the tongue increasing slowly with a good mouth feel, lightly oily with a very light sweetness of grain. The aftertaste is almost non-existent, with a very light feel of grainy sweetness, a light burn to the back of the throat and tongue upon swallowing and a very clean mouth feel that dissipates slowly.

Grey Goose Vodka, 80 proof (France)

Clear and clean, with some chatoyance, good viscosity and long legs leaving very tiny droplets after slipping down the side of the glass. The first nosing reveals a good amount of alcohol burn to the nasal passages and a light caramelly mustiness. The second pass brings less alcohol and also less of any other aromas, but there is an increase of the mustiness on the third pass. The first sip is almost neutral with some inherent sweetness becoming evident, and a light feel of alcohol bringing a tingle to the tip of the tongue. Very neutral in overall flavor with a light grainy sweetness in the aftertaste which brings out a smooth light caramel finish and more burn.

Hertekamp Vodka (Belgium)

Bright and clean, colorless, good legs. Citrus nose, lightly acidic, light burn in nasal passages. Sweet medium burn to center of tongue, lightly chewy, sweet finish with mellow aftertaste and no burn to throat.

Ketel One Vodka, 80 proof (Holland)

Very clean and bright, almost flashing as it reflects light and good viscosity with long legs. smooth sheeting action which leaves medium sized droplets on the side of the glass. The first nosing reveals a neutral nose with little alcohol burn to the nasal passages. On subsequent sniffs, the alcohol burn increases but little else changes and I couldn't detect any aromas that shouldn't be there. The first sip is light with some grainy sweetness and very little burn. There is a very clean mouth feel with more alcohol present in the second sip and the sweetness still there. The aftertaste is bright and pleasantly sweet with a little alcohol burn which fades to a long finish and a neutral end. Ketel One is a truly excellent vodka, fairly neutral in taste, with few distracting congeners.

Mezzaluna Vodka, 80 proof (Italy)

Clear and clean with a very light hint of beige color; good slender legs. A hint of sweet toffee in the nose with a touch of acetone and little nasal burn. There's a definite sweetness to the tongue with strong burn in the mouth and a good citrus feel. The aftertaste is sweet with more than a hint of tart lemon and a long finish. A little water brings out the citrus to the nose and the palate even more strongly.

Though marketed as a plain vodka, Mezzaluna could easily have been listed as a flavored vodka, because of the prominent lemon flavor. However you classify it, it's a well-structured and rewarding taste experience.

Rigalya Baltic Vodka, 80 proof (Latvia)

Clean and clear with a hint of beige in color, decent viscosity and long legs. The first nosing reveals a very faint hint of toffee, with a light alcohol attack to the sinuses and further sniffs reveal nothing new. The first sip is light in the mouth, slightly sweet and attacks the center of the tongue and the back of the throat with a light burn. The second sip is even sweeter with a steadily increasing burn to the center of the tongue and along the edges until the mouth is filled with the sweetness of the vodka. The aftertaste is smooth and sweet, with a light burn which ebbs slowly and dies through the long finish until the sweet end. Adding a little water brings out a mustiness to the nose and a light oiliness in the mouth.

Royalty Vodka (The Netherlands)

Clean and bright with good legs and light viscosity. Light alcohol nose with no off aromas and a light burn to the sinuses. Smooth sweetness, with a medium attack to the center and front of the tongue with some burn to the roof of the mouth, lightly chewy. The aftertaste is light with some tingle to the palate and a sweetish feel that slowly fades to a clean light finish.

Sundsvall Vodka, 80 proof (Sweden)

Clear, clean, and bright with no color and good legs. A little chalk to the nose but fairly neutral and a feel of charcoal with no nasal burn. The first sip is a little hot and grows warmer in the mouth with a definite sweetness and a light oily mouth feel. The aftertaste starts dry, turning to slightly sweet, and the finish is long and fairly neutral. Adding water yields no further aromas though it makes the mouth feel a little rubbery, bringing out a charcoal tang.

Tanqueray Sterling Vodka (England)

Clean and bright with good viscosity, long legs, and a smooth sheeting action. A pale greyish color is present when held up against white paper. The first nosing reveals a neutral state with very little alcohol burn. Deeper sniffs bring more burn but no change in aromas. The first sip shows a little alcohol attack to the center of the tongue and a very faint sweetness mainly concentrated in the front of the mouth. A clean aftertaste with a faintly sweet long finish ebbs to a neutral state of flavor and leaves only a certain crispness. Adding a little water brings out no further aromas but does enhance the sweetness.

Van Hoo Vodka, 80 proof (Belgium)

Clear and clean, no color, and some chatoyance with good legs. The first nosing shows citrus zest with a light nasal burn. In the mouth there is an initial burn which swiftly mellows to a tingle to the center of the tongue. A slight oiliness but little chewiness and an overall sweetness throughout the taste, with an aftertaste which starts out sweet and then turns clean and has a long finish.

Vodka Monopolowa, 80 proof (Austria)

A potato vodka. Clear and clean with long medium thick legs. A very light acetone nose with a very strong alcohol burn to the nasal passages. The first sip is very clean with some inherent sweetness and very little burn to the tongue or the palate. Slightly oily and a little chewy with good mouth feel. A very light aftertaste and a medium finish. Overall, much like a metal covered with silk. The second sip reveals a little more burn to the tongue but still very clean with a light citric flavor.

Zelta Vodka, 80 proof (Latvia)

Clear and clean with long legs. A hint of mint and citrus, more lime than lemon in the nose with a medium burn in the sinuses. The first sip is very smooth with almost no flavor and no burn in the mouth, just a little heat at the back of the throat when you swallow. Not sweet but slightly acrid in the aftertaste, with a finish that is very long and turns slightly sweet just before it fades into nothingness.

Polish Vodkas

Belvedere Vodka, 80 proof

Made from Polish rye grain. Very clear and bright, with long slender legs. Mellow, slightly musty nose with little nasal burn and no off aromas. Slightly sweet and chewy, with an oily feel and light burn to the front of the mouth. A good sweet aftertaste with a long finish that leaves a light sweetness on the palate.

Chopin Vodka, 80 proof

Made from Stobrawa Potatoes. Clear and clean with a very light gray tint, long, heavy legs and good viscosity. Smooth, mellow nose with a medium nasal burn and a light caramel aroma. In the mouth there is a sweetish, lightly oily feel with a medium burn to the front of the mouth and a toffee taste leading to the aftertaste which is even sweeter than the first impression and has a medium burn in the long finish which eases to a sigh of mellowness. A superb representative of the Polish-style vodkas, clean and light but with that elusive extra 'something'.

CK Vodka, 80 proof (Lancut Distillery)

Clear and clean with no color and long, slender legs. The nose reveals little aroma except a light alcohol and no nasal burn. In the mouth there is a little oiliness, almost no flavor and a light burn to the front of the mouth with a smooth sweetness. The aftertaste shows a light alcohol flavor and a long light finish with no burn. Very nice.

Krolewska Vodka. 80 proof

Made from Polish grain. Clear and clean with no color and long, medium legs, a light, grainy nose with both a very light toffee and even lighter acetone nose and a light nasal burn. In the mouth it shows a medium burn with some oiliness and is lightly chewy and shows some sweet grain taste. The aftertaste is sweetly pleasant with a long finish which turns almost but not quite dry.

Luksusowa, 80 proof

A potato vodka, clear and clean with just a hint of beige with clean unbroken legs and smooth drainage. To the nose there is a light caramelly aroma of sugar with a strong alcohol burn to the nasal passages. In the mouth there is an inherent sweetness, light oiliness and slightly chewy with some burn to the center of the tongue. The aftertaste shows a metallic sting with less sweetness and no alcohol burn to the throat and a long mainly neutral finish.

Original Polish, 80 proof

Made from the shaft of rye. Clear and clean with no hint of color, good viscosity and long, slender legs. A light caramel nose is evident with a light mellow burn to the nasal passages. In the mouth it is very pleasant with a medium burn to the front of the tongue and the lips which moves back to the center of the tongue. It is slightly oily and mildly chewy with a smooth slide down the throat leaving a mildly sweet aftertaste and a long finish.

Polonaise Polish Vodka, 80 proof

Clear and clean with no color and long, slender legs. A slight mustiness in the nose with a light burn and no off odors. Inherently sweet in the mouth with a light oiliness and a little burn to the front of the tongue and inside the lips. The aftertaste is sweet with a very light tang of citrus and a long, dry finish with a light burn to the throat as it goes down.

Posejdon Potato Vodka, 80 proof

Made from potatoes. Clear and clean with long, medium-width legs and medium viscosity. Almost no aroma with a mild nasal burn. The mouth shows a light burn and a steel/silver taste with slight potato sweetness. The aftertaste holds to the sweetness and has a long finish with a light potato sting at the end.

Wodka Wyborowa, 80 proof

Made from 100 percent neutral grain spirits. Clear and clean with a very light brown tint and medium thick short legs. The nose is steely and dry with light nasal burn and no discernible off aromas. In the mouth there is an initial sweetness with a light burn to the center of the upper palate and a light oily feel, no chewiness and a clean, slightly herbal aftertaste, and a long finish.

Extra Zytnia, 80 proof

Clear and clean to the eye with long, slender legs and a very light pale brown color. A very light fruit aroma with medium nasal burn and no off scents. Definitely sweet in the mouth with some burn to the front of the tongue and a bright bite to the inside of the mouth. Almost crisp. The aftertaste is pleasant and long with a slight tang to the finish leaving the mouth feeling slightly dry. Adding water allows the fruit flavors to come to the front a little more, and brings out other flavors.

Russian, Ukrainian, and Belorussian Vodkas

Charodei Vodka, 80 proof (Belorus)

Clear and clean with long, slender legs, and just a hint of color. No off aromas but a medium nasal burn. The first sip shows a natural sweetness and some burn to the tongue, chewy with a little oiliness, a pleasant, lightly sweet aftertaste with a long finish and a concluding sting of alcohol to the palate.

Kremlovskaya Vodka, 80 proof (Russia)

Clear and clean with long, slender, evenly arranged legs and no color. No off aromas but a medium nasal burn. In the mouth there is a light oiliness, not much chewiness, and a good, slightly sweet mouth feel with a little burn to the front edges of the tongue. A sweet aftertaste with a little metal undertone and a medium to long finish. This vodka has something of a traditional style and preserves some congeners that I found added depth and interest.

Old Kiev, 80 proof (Ukraine)

Clean and clear with many long legs. A slight licorice or anise nose with some acetone and a light nasal burn. In the mouth there is some burn and a slight taste of chocolate, little oil, slightly sweet, rather clean and not chewy. The aftertaste is sweet with a little burn to the rear of the palate and long lasting with a neutral finish.

Priviet Vodka, 80 proof (Russia)

Clear and clean, no color, with long slender legs. A hint of toffee in the first nosing with a light alcohol nasal burn. Very clean in the mouth with a light citric feel, some oiliness, and a little chewy. Good mouth feel with an inherent dryness to the overall taste, very little burn in the mouth, and a pleasant aftertaste with a long finish.

Smirnoff Black Label, 80 proof (Russia)

Very clean and bright with no color, medium length, and thickness in the legs. A very light vegetative aroma at the first nosing, slightly sweet, deeper nosings show a light cabbage aroma with a little nasal burn. Slightly oily in the mouth with a medium burn to the front and center of the tongue and lightly chewy. A light burn in the pleasantly sweet aftertaste with a long lasting finish.

Staraya Moskva, 80 proof (Russia)

Clear with a hint of brown color, short and thin legs with light viscosity. The nose is terrible, like rotten cabbage or spoiled kimchee, with overtones of acetone and a harsh alcohol nasal burn. The first sip is metallic and unpleasant, with some sweetness and a medium burn to the center of the tongue. The aftertaste is sweetish and medium in length with a slightly off finish

Stolichnaya, 80 proof (Russia)

Clear and clean, no color, good viscosity, and long legs. The first nosing reveals a light acetone with a musty vegetable overlay and a medium nasal burn. In the mouth it is clean with some sweetness and an increasing heat to the center of the tongue, lightly oily, and medium chewy. The aftertaste reveals a burst of sweetness which slowly dries out to a long, sweetly citric finish.

Stolichnaya Gold, 80 proof (Russia)

Clean and bright, no color, very smooth sheeting action and very long legs. The first nosing reveals a hint of something difficult to describe, not unpleasant, but not quite normal, with a light nasal burn. In the mouth there is little burn at first but some tingle to the center of the tongue. There is some oiliness and it is lightly chewy with a slight sweetness to the aftertaste and a good, long finish.

St. Petersburg Vodka, 80 proof (Russia)

Clear and clean to the eye with a very light beige tinge and long, slender legs. To the nose there is a light caramel aroma and some acetone with little nasal burn. In the mouth it is very light with a growing presence and some heat to the center of the tongue. The aftertaste has a metallic steel taste and is slightly sweet but not unpleasant and shows a long finish.

Volganaya Vodka, 80 proof (Russia)

Clear and bright with no color, good viscosity, and very good legs. The first nosing has a very light caramel nose with a medium nasal burn. In the mouth there is a metallic first nip with a light burn to the tip of the tongue spreading to the top of the soft palate. A light oiliness and lightly chewy with a slightly sweet aftertaste leading to a long finish.

The Rest of the World

Cane Spirit Rothschild (St. Kitts)

Absolutely clear and clean, with no color, and very slow-moving, long, slender legs. In the nose the aroma is of a very light toffee and some alcohol burn to the nasal passages. In the mouth the spirit begins sweet with a smooth burn to the tongue, slightly chewy, a light oiliness and clean flavor. The aftertaste is sweet with a little charcoal, very little burn to the throat and a long sweet finish.

Exclusiv Vodka, 80 proof (Puerto Rico)

Made in Puerto Rico, this can be viewed as a Caribbean or an American vodka. Clean, with a very light hint of beige and long medium-thick legs. The nose shows a clean light nasal burn with just a hint of toffee and a little chocolate. The first sip shows a stronger chocolate flavor with some oiliness and is lightly chewy. There is little burn in the mouth and the total effect is sweet and smooth. The aftertaste is still sweet and has a long, sweet finish.

Jinro Shochu, 48 proof (Korea)

Clean and clear, with a light greyish tint and no legs. It slides down the side of the glass, all in one piece. To the nose there is no burn with just a little alcohol and lemon scents. In the mouth there is a slight steel flavor with overtones of citrus. The overall feel is almost neutral, with no burn and little taste. The aftertaste shows the citrus and a very light sweetness that has a surprisingly long finish.

Aquavits

These two aquavits were impressively made, but did not move me. I think it all depends upon your subjective response to the flavor of caraway.

Aalborg Akvavit, 80 proof (Denmark)

Clear and clean, with no color, and broken, long legs. In the nose it displays almost an aniseed character with a light burn to the nasal passages and the characteristic caraway feel. In the mouth it has a burnt steel dryness and some burn to the back of the throat which slowly modifies itself to sweetness and a caraway flavor and some oiliness. The aftertaste is cloying with some sweetness and the caraway taste continues through the long finish.

Linie Aquavit, 83 proof (Norway)

A light beige in color in the glass, it's darker in the bottle and shows medium broken legs. Very pungent in the nose with a good nasal burn and an aniseed undertone to add to the caraway punch. Sweet to the tongue with the caraway pungency still present and slightly oily with a light to medium burn to the front part of the tongue. The aftertaste reveals the caraway even more strongly, as though eating a piece of buttered New York rye toast. Little to no burn going down with a long finish and a remaining taste of the caraway.

Flavored Vodkas

Absolut Citron, 80 proof

Clear and clean, with no color, and long, slender legs. A good nose of citron, both orange and lemon are present with a mild nasal burn. In the mouth there is a mild citric feel with a medium burn to the tongue and the palate, plus some oiliness. The aftertaste is pleasantly sweet and clean with a definite citric feel and a long sweet aftertaste.

Absolut Kurant, 80 proof

Clear and clean, with no color and broken legs. The nose reveals a strong berry or currant aroma which overpowers any other scents and has a mild nasal burn. In the mouth there is a definite currant taste with a mild alcohol burn to the tongue. The aftertaste is lightly tart with some inherent sweetness and a long finish.

Absolut Peppar, 80 proof

Clear and clean, with no color and long slender legs. To the nose there is a mustiness that could be related to the pepper used in the vodka and it smells more like bell peppers than hot peppers. No other aromas are evident and no nasal burn was found. In the mouth there is a light feel of bell pepper, slightly sweet, with a little burn to the tongue, both pepper heat and alcohol heat. The aftertaste shows a medium pepper burn to the throat with a mild, long finish.

Finlandia Cranberry, 60 proof

Clean, with no foreign objects, a red-orange color, and long, slender legs. To the nose there is a light cranberry tang which is the only discernible component of the aroma. In the mouth there is a medium cranberry tang but still a strong alcohol burn is evident to the tongue and palate. The aftertaste shows a sweet tang and a certain tartness with a good medium finish.

Gordon's Citrus, 70 proof

Clean and clear, with no color, and good, slender legs. The nose reveals light citrus aromas, mainly lime, and a medium nasal burn. In the mouth there is little feel of any thing other than a very light citric taste with a medium alcohol burn to the tongue. The aftertaste shows a little more citrus with little throat burn and a long finish. Not a real favorite of mine, but it could be a decent mixer.

Gordon's Orange, 60 proof

Clear and clean, with no color, and good, medium legs. To the nose there is a definite orange aroma but also a hint of bitterness as if there had been pith in the squeeze, imparting a not very pleasant but very definite orange scent, and no nasal burn. In the mouth there is a strong, sweet orange flavor with a little tang and some burn to the tongue. The aftertaste has a citrus feel but there is a slight bitterness and an unidentifiable flavor that slowly ebbs in a long finish. Should be a good mixer.

Gordon's Wildberry, 60 proof

Clear and clean, with no color, and good, slender legs. The nose reveals an almost overpowering combination of cranberry and some other berry scents that have a slightly acrid smell like an extremely potent Kool-Aid, hiding anything else that might be present. In the mouth the nose is not borne out, the berry flavor is not so overpowering, though still strong enough to hide other flavors. The aftertaste is still lighter and is quite acceptable, with almost no burn and a slight sweetness. I can't think of a cocktail which this vodka would enhance, and can't imagine *anyone* wanting to drink it straight. Definitely not to my taste.

Inferno Pepper Vodka, 78.6 proof

Clear and clean, with just a hint of reddish-brown color, very slender legs that leave tiny droplets on the side of the glass. The pepper is very evident in the nose, though it has more of a bell pepper than hot pepper aroma. There are no other discernible aromas and little alcohol burn to the nasal passages. In the mouth it is hot, though not distressingly so, and the pepper flavor seems to deaden the tongue a little. The aftertaste is pepper hot and because of that the finish is long. The vodka is not unpleasant, but the main characteristic is indisputably the pepper and there is little else to distinguish it.

Kremlovskaya Chocolate, 80 proof

Clear and clean, with no color, and long, slender legs. The nose shows a good aroma of bittersweet chocolate and a light nasal alcohol burn. In the mouth there is a light flavor of chocolate which grows stronger and more evident the longer it is held in the mouth, with a medium alcohol burn to the tongue. The aftertaste is chocolaty and mildly sweet with a long pleasant finish. A surprising success, and a real treat to drink straight. Remarkable how nearly everyone likes this so much more than they expected they would.

Kremlovskaya Limonnaya, 80 proof

Clear and clean, with no color, and long, slender legs. The nose is light and lemony with no other detectable aromas and a slight nasal burn. The taste shows light lemon with a little burn to the center of the tongue and no other tastes except a little alcohol. The aftertaste reveals a lemon tang with a little natural sweetness and a light long clean finish. Overall, a smooth tangy tipple which can be used in almost any cocktail. Probably the most successful combination of vodka and citrus on the market.

Smirnoff Citrus Twist, 70 proof

Clear and clean, with no color, and long, medium-width legs. The nose is slightly citric but the individual fruit is not discernible, just an overall citrus feel with possibly some grapefruit and a little lime. In the mouth the citrus is certainly present but again is more of a blended feel than any specific fruit, with a light alcohol burn to the tongue. The aftertaste reveals a slight sweetness with a tangy lime overtone and a long finish.

Stolichnaya Cinnamon (Zinamon), 70 proof

Clear and clean, with just a hint of brown, and long, slender legs. A good cinnamon nose, tingly with a little heat, a light bite of cinnamon, and no alcohol nasal burn. In the mouth there is a smooth feel of cinnamon but no heat and no burn anywhere in the mouth. The aftertaste shows just a spicy tang of the cinnamon and a long, slightly sweet, spicy finish. I would like a little more cinnamon, but the overall balance is very good.

Stolichnaya Coffee (Kafka), 70 proof

Clear and clean, with no color and long medium-width legs. To the nose there is a definite coffee-bean aroma, fresh and slightly biting, which no other aromas can penetrate, and no alcohol burn. In the mouth there is a smooth flavor which isn't quite what I expected; the coffee has a good taste but I find a little citrus in the flavor and it is not quite a true coffee feel. The aftertaste is fairly neutral with just a little coffee, no alcohol feel at all, and a clean, mild finish. There is no sweetness in this spirit and it will impart just a hint of coffee to whatever you mix it with. Again I would like more coffee flavor and find the overall feel a little bland.

Stolichnaya Lemon (Limonnaya), 80 proof

Clear and clean, with just a hint of very light beige color, and long, wide legs. The nose shows citrus but some bitterness and tang without a definite lemon aroma, more as if the pith of the lemon were used rather than the zest, and there is a light alcohol nasal burn. In the mouth there is a sweet lemony flavor with some alcohol burn and no other discernible flavors. The aftertaste has a light lemon tang with a hint of something akin to fish, and the finish is not long.

Stolichnaya Okhotnichya (Herbal with Honey), 90 proof

This is called 'Hunter's Vodka'. Clean, with a reddish-gold amber color, no particles and long, very slender legs. To the nose there is a definite herbal feel with a light vegetative undertone and the honey can be sensed with little alcohol nasal burn. In the mouth there is a medium burn to the tongue and palate, and a sweet herb flavor through which no other tastes can be detected. The aftertaste shows a herbal tang with a light peppery feel and a long, fairly dry finish.

Stolichnaya Orange (Ohranj), 70 proof

Clear and clean, with no color and long, slender legs. The nose reveals sweet orange aromas with a light bitter undertone and no nasal burn. In the mouth there is an orange feel with a medium alcohol burn to the center of the tongue and no other detectable flavors. The aftertaste shows an even more bitter feel with the dominant orange over-riding all other flavors and a long finish.

Stolichnaya Peach (Persik), 70 proof

Clear and clean with just a hint of beige and long medium-width legs. The nose reveals a rich peach aroma with a nice peachy tang and no nasal burn as though you were smelling the outside of a ripe peach. In the mouth the aroma is a little disappointing, as the taste doesn't quite live up to the beginning of the aroma. The aftertaste shows a peachy feel with a little alcohol and a long finish. The nose is wonderful, I just wish it followed through in the mouth.

Stolichnaya Pertsovka (Pepper), 70 proof

Clean, with a yellow orange amber color, no particulate matter, and long slender legs. The nose reveals a peppery herbal feel not unlike the Okhotnichya with no nasal burn. In the mouth there is quite a lot of pepper heat to the entire mouth, but the tongue brings more as the spirit rests in the mouth with no herbs to soften the flavor. The aftertaste shows a peppery burn down the throat and has a good medium heat, with a long finish.

Stolichnaya Raspberry (Razberi), 70 proof

Clear and clean, with no color and long, broken legs. The raspberry nose is very strong with the slight bitterness you would expect from a raspberry liqueur, no other aromas, and little nasal burn. In the mouth there is a good berry flavor with no off tastes and a medium burn to the tongue and lips. The aftertaste shows a sweet sting down the throat and a long warm finish.

Stolichnaya Strawberry (Strasberi), 70 proof

Clean and clear, with no color and lots of slender legs. The nose shows a musty strawberry aroma, as if the berries weren't quite ripe, and no other scents are discernible. In the mouth there is a light strawberry taste that slowly grows stronger and a medium alcohol burn is present throughout the interior. The aftertaste shows a light berry taste, with a little throat burn, and a long finish.

Stolichnaya Vanilla (Vanil), 70 proof

Clean and bright, with no color, and long, slender legs. The nose shows some light vanilla with an unknown undertone and a light nasal burn (the nose could be much richer in this spirit). The mouth reveals a little better vanilla flavor with some alcohol burn to the tongue and no other flavors. The aftertaste shows a little heat to the throat, a light vanilla feel, and a long finish.

Wyborowa Lemon, 76 proof

Clear and clean, with a hint of gray, and long, slender, broken legs. The nose reveals a good puckery lemon aroma with just a hint of bitterness and a medium alcohol nasal burn. In the mouth there is a little lemon flavor with an alcohol burn to the lips and tongue and just a little bitterness. The aftertaste shows a strong alcohol impact with some lemon and more bitterness over an underlying sweetness.

Wyborowa Orange, 76 proof

Clear and clean, with a hint of gray, and long broken legs. The nose reveals a light orange scent with a strong alcohol nasal burn that covers any other aromas. In the mouth there is an alcohol attack to the lips and center of the tongue with an inherent sweetness and a light orange flavor. The aftertaste has again the light flavor of orange but almost none of the alcohol burn you would expect, and a light medium finish.

Wyborowa Pineapple, 76 proof

Clear and clean, with little color and broken legs. The nose shows a strong pineapple aroma with the tang you would expect from that fruit and almost no alcohol burn. In the mouth there is a strong alcohol burn with a good pineapple flavor and almost no other tastes and a slight bitterness. The aftertaste shows some burn down the throat with a nice pineapple tang which last through the long finish.

Zubrowka Bison Grass Vodka, 80 proof

Clear and clean, with long slender legs. In the nose there is a light grassy aroma with some nasal burn and a light caramel feel. In the mouth there is a definite sweetness with a light burn throughout the mouth and a unique spicy flavor which I can only say must come from the bison grass, for it is unlike any other vodka flavor I have experienced. The aftertaste shows the same spiciness with a light hint of cinnamon and very little burn down the throat. Zubrowka offers something unusual yet delightful, a successful repositioning of a traditional flavoring element.

Vodka Liqueurs

Keglevich Forestberries, 40 proof (Trieste, Italy)

No visible particulate matter, but a little cloudy and a rich reddish brown color that shows some legs and slow drainage. The nose shows mainly raspberry or others of the bramble sort, blackberry or boysenberry, with some light alcohol nasal burn. The mouth reveals a sweet tartness with little alcohol and any other flavors covered by the berries. The aftertaste shows good sweet berry flavor with the same tartness and no alcohol in the throat.

Keglevich Lemon, 40 proof (Trieste, Italy)

Clear and clean, with no color and long wide legs. The nose shows a strong lemon tang with a soapy scent and a little alcohol nasal burn. In the mouth the dry lemon taste is well balanced with a very light sweetness and a clean tang with little alcohol burn. The aftertaste shows some sweetness with the soapy feel even stronger than the nose and no burn to the throat.

Keglevich Melon, 40 proof (Trieste, Italy)

Clean, with a hint of gray and long, wide legs. The nose has some melon, mainly honeydew with a soapy feel and sticky sweet aroma and no nasal burn. The mouth shows a sweet honeydew flavor with a little alcohol sting to the tip of the tongue and no other flavors. The aftertaste shows a sweet cloying melon taste with some soap and a long sweet finish.

Keglevich Peach, 40 proof (Trieste, Italy)

Clear and clean, with just a hint of greyish-brown and wide broken legs. The nose shows the peach to be very rich and mouth-watering with no other scents and a little nasal alcohol burn. The mouth shows a rich, sweet peach flavor with a little bitterness, no other flavors, and some alcohol burn. The aftertaste is very peachy with a fuzzy sweetness, no alcohol burn and a very long, sweet finish.

Keglevich Strawberry, 40 proof (Trieste, Italy)

No obvious particulate matter but slightly cloudy and a dark reddish-brown color with decent legs. The nose has a certain tang that has a little mustiness but not what I can recognize as being strawberry, it actually smells much like a fortified wine such as Pineau des Charentes, with no nasal burn. The mouth also has more the feel of a Pineau des Charentes and I cannot recognize the strawberry taste, but there is a little alcohol sting to the lips. The aftertaste is sweet and shows more berry flavor with little burn to the throat and a sweet long finish.

Krupnik Polish Honey Liqueur, 80 proof (Poland)

A clear deep golden color, with long, medium legs. A complex mixture of aromas with cloves and other spices evident and little nasal burn. Very sweet and honey-like in the mouth with good complexity and lightly oily, some burn to the soft palate and the front of the tongue. The aftertaste has a light burn that smoothes out and becomes very nicely sweet with an undertone of bitter. The finish is long and sweet but not overly so. Krupnik is the best vodka liqueur I know of.

Zone Peach, 50 proof

Clear and clean, with no color and long, medium-width legs. The nose reveals a luscious peach aroma with a hint of nectarine tang, no other discernible scents and almost no nasal alcohol burn. In the mouth there is still a luscious peach flavor with more alcohol and an inherent sweet tang. The aftertaste shows a good peach flavor and a little sting from the alcohol, with a slight bitterness underlying the sweetness of the overall taste.

6
A Little Vodka History

A fire broke out in a village; there was a church in the village, but the tavernkeeper came out and shouted that if the villagers abandoned the church and saved his tavern, he would stand them a barrel of vodka. The church burned down, but the tavern was saved.

Fyodor Dostoievsky, *A Writer's Diary*

A few years ago an argument flared up between Poles and Russians over who had the right of prior use for the name 'vodka'. The Polish vodka manufacturers were attempting to prove that they had prior rights since, they claimed, their version of vodka predated that of Russia.

The Poles maintained that 'gorzalka' (Polish for vodka), had been in production since the twelfth century. The Russians disputed this and put a linguist and historian named Pokhlebkin onto the problem. Pokhlebkin's *History of Vodka* (published in English in 1992) is quite persuasive, but there will always be doubts about allegations of one-sided priority in a region like Eastern Europe. One of Pokhlebkin's claims is that the Poles had been put up to this challenge by the Western liquor companies who wanted to claim rights to the name 'vodka' through the Poles and block out the Russian rights to that name. But 'vodka' is undoubtedly a Russian word (it means 'little water'), and it has become the recognized international name for a definite type of spirit to which 'gorzalka' belongs.

The initial development of the distilled spirit that is today known as 'vodka' was made somewhere in eastern Europe. This region has been fought over, conquered, and reconquered so many times by so many differing social and political groups that the ethnic identity of the particular group of people who actually invented the first version of vodka may never be known.

The Invention of Distilling

In any case, distillation was invented, or re-invented, in the East and brought to the West. Although the ancient Egyptians, Greeks, and Romans may well have known something about distilling, there is no dispute that, if they did, this knowledge completely died out in Europe during the Dark Ages. Distillation was brought to Europe in the tenth century by the Moors, who ultimately learned it from China. Therefore distillation could easily have entered Eastern Europe by more than one route, and could have come into Poland and Russia independently at about the same time.

Wine and beer are the earliest alcoholic drinks. Wine has been made and consumed for at least eight thousand, and beer for at least seven thousand, years. Producing these beverages makes use of the natural process of fermentation, which often occurs without human intervention, and which automatically creates a small amount of alcohol in a fluid that is mostly water.

Distillation is a method of concentrating the alcohol produced by fermentation. After this technique was brought into Europe by the Moors, its spread was slow, being brought from Spain to Ireland by traveling monks. After distillation had taken root in Ireland, it soon spread to Scotland. From early times, distillation has also been applied for purposes other than drink production, being employed, for example, by French perfumiers to fix the essences of various flowers, and by physicians who wanted concentrated alcohol as an antiseptic for wounds.

The Slavs Colonize Eastern Europe

In ancient times Eastern Europe was dominated by tribes of warlike nomads, such as the Cimmerians and the Scythians. During the first 600 years following the changing of the era, nomadic tribes like the Sarmatians, Goths, Huns, and Avars ruled over the plains of Eastern Europe. Each ruled in their own time until they were displaced by the next tribe of invaders come to conquer this land of endless steppes.

At some time before 600 C.E. the land began to be occupied by tribes of Slavic peoples who were not nomads, but settlers who farmed the land more intensively and were less likely to move on. The Slavs eventually separated into three peoples: the East Slavs, who became the Russians, Ukrainians, and Belorussians; the West Slavs, who became Poles and Czechs; and the South Slavs, who became Serbs and Bulgarians.

The Mongol Conquest

The first of the major Slavic kingdoms was the Kievan State. Beginning around 882 C.E. this political state went through the normal groups of rulers and endured until 1240 when the Mongols came and conquered all the peoples living on the open steppes.

One of the reasons that the Mongol conquest was so quick was that the Slavic states tended to fragment, with the division of each kingdom among the king's sons upon his death. The Mongols easily defeated the numerous small quarrelsome kingdoms and city-states, setting up a centralized state called 'The Golden Horde', based on the Volga river.

During the time the Russians today still refer to as 'The Tatar Yoke', the Mongols (or Tatars) actually reigned over the area quite lightly. Those princes who bowed their heads to their new Mongol masters were allowed to keep their thrones, as long as they showed due respect to the Tatars and paid the annual tribute of treasure. Of all of the Slavic princes whose holdings were in the area, there was always one prince that the Mongols would designate as the 'Great Prince'. This Prince would become the main administrator of the area under Mongol control, responsible for the collection of taxes, most of which were handed over to the Mongol overlords.

While the Russians were in subjection to the Mongols, the Polish state was prospering and growing. During the fourteenth century, the northern kingdom of Lithuania emerged as one of the powers in Eastern Europe, and came to control a large portion of what had been Kievan Russia, including the entire Dnieper valley. Over the next 200 years this state forged a strong alliance with Poland, beginning with a marriage between the ruling families in 1386 and culminating with the actual merger of Poland and Lithuania in the Union of Lublin in 1569. The areas of old Russia controlled by the Polish-Lithuanian government are now called Ukraine and Belorus, and the areas that were under the Tatar Yoke are now called Russia.

Many battles between the Russian peoples and the combined nations of the Poles and the Lithuanians pushed the western boundaries of Russia back and forth during the fourteenth and fifteenth centuries. But eventually it became clear that the city-state of Moscow was growing in power over the Russians. The prince of Moscow was recognized by the Mongols as the Great Prince. Then, in 1452, Ivan III (the Great) threw off the Mongol overlordship, and tribute was no longer paid. Some Russian historians claim that vodka was originally developed around this time.

Some Poles claim that Poles had developed 'gorzalka' as early the 1100s. (Actually, some have claimed a date in the eighth century!) Well, they may have used the old technique of allowing wine to freeze and then casting off the ice to increase the alcoholic strength, but the actual art of distillation by heating and condensation probably didn't reach Poland until after 1400. The first written reference may be in a source dated 1405. Some Polish historians claim that this is the earliest reference to vodka in the whole of Eastern Europe. There is a more certain reference to Polish vodka in a herbal book of 1534.

Western Catholics and Eastern Orthodox

Distilling must certainly have been established in Italy before it reached Eastern Europe. A Genoese delegation visited the Lithuanian court in 1426 and demonstrated distilling techniques. The Poles also claim that the word 'vodka' and the concept of distillation reached Russia from the west, coming through Lithuania and the other countries which touch on both Poland and Russia.

The Russians claim that probably the first vodka distilled in the region was made by one of the monks of the Orthodox Church following a trip to Italy in the late 1430s to attend the Eighth Ecumenical Council of the Roman Catholic church. Monks and priests of the church were the best educated of all of the peoples of the area at the time and they were sure to have been exposed to the art of distillation practiced in the Italian monasteries.

In both Catholic and Orthodox countries, priests and monks tended to be the repositories of knowledge, and distillation of spirits was no exception. Various orders within the Roman Catholic church have made liquor for centuries. For example, both the Benedictine and Chartreuse liqueurs were begun by orders of the Catholic Church. (The Carthusian order is still involved in the manufacture of 'Chartreuse', but Benedictine has become a separate commercial enterprise, with no further involvement by the Benedictine order.)

There is some evidence that the man who actually helped develop distillation as well as teaching it to the Slavs may have been one Isidor, a Greek from

Thessalonia who, after his return from a journey to Italy, was imprisoned in the Chudov monastery. He spent a year there before fleeing to Kiev and from there back to Rome.

The Expansion of Russia

Following the defeat of the Mongols by Moscow, more and more Russian city-states came under Moscow's control. Under leaders like Ivan IV (the Terrible), and Boris Godunov, Moscow continued to expand, and the prince became more powerful, adopting the title 'tsar', from the Latin imperial name 'Caesar'.

Vodka played a major role in the lives of the people and in the system of government. It was one of the main sources of taxation revenue for the tsar and his court. At certain times, it has been estimated, more than half the income of the government came from taxes on vodka, including grants of monopoly to produce vodka.

While the tsars indulged in prolonged conflict with Poland and Lithuania, they also started a long running conflict with a political grouping along the Baltic coast called 'Livonian Order'. These descendants of a medieval order of knights ruled over a considerable part of the Baltic coast, in alliance with the archbishop of Riga and certain individual city-states, blocking Ivan IV from one of his great dreams, a port on the Baltic Sea which would give Russia easier access to western trade. The war against these and other groups in the area dragged on for some time and Russia and her tsars became ever more deeply absorbed in their quest for more land and power.

In the period from 1598 to 1613, now called 'The Time of Troubles', there was a continuous civil war inside Russia. The convoluted story, involving the intrigues of the Lithuanian and Polish Roman Catholics, is related in Mussorgsky's wonderful opera, *Boris Godunov* (whose early tavern scene indicates the importance of vodka in the social life of the country). After two Polish invasions, the then very powerful Swedes also invaded, and the Russians would undoubtedly have accepted Wladyslaw, the new Swedish tsar imposed upon them, if only his father, the Swedish king Sigismund, had kept his promise that Wladyslaw would abandon Rome and adhere to Orthodoxy. When it became clear that Wladyslaw would remain a Papist, Russia fell into chaos and was again invaded by Poland.

In 1611, the Russian Orthodox church got together a couple of armies and finally drove out the Poles, retaking Moscow in the fall of 1612. In 1613, the 'Time of Troubles' ended with the selection of a new tsar. Michael Romanov was crowned tsar after being selected by the *zemskii sobor*, a parliament composed of aristocratic boyars and influential members of the common people, plus some advice from the clergy. The Romanovs remained the royal house until 1917.

Oppression of the Peasants

Down through the centuries, the lives of the people and the development of vodka went hand in hand. But vodka could be produced only under a monopoly grant from the tsar, and all aspects of vodka production were regulated by the tsar.

To help the big landowners, the tsar enacted laws binding the peasants to the land, and these restrictions steadily became worse. Eventually the peasant became a serf, virtually a slave. The serfs had the consolation of vodka, though the vodka they drank was of a very inferior sort. The aristocrats and boyars drank the finest vodka, which could rival the best brandies and other spirits in the world at that time, but the vodka served to the peasants and serfs was made by the cheapest methods.

A very corrupt system prevailed in which the manufacture and sale of vodka were controlled by men appointed as keepers of the tsar's taverns. The vodka itself contained hazardous substances because of the inefficiency of distillation, and the bad aromas and tastes could only be hidden by the addition of various flavorings. This vodka often left the consumer feeling weak and caused terrible hangovers due to its residual fusel oils and other unpleasant chemicals.

As in Western Europe and colonial America at the time, consumption of alcohol by the ordinary people was enormous by comparison with later levels. The standard measure used to sell vodka in Russia from the beginning of distillation to the invention of the bottle, was the bucket, which varied between twelve and fourteen liters, finally becoming stabilized at twelve liters in 1621. A peasant bought his vodka in a bucket and took home twelve liters (over three gallons), for his family's normal consumption.

The Flourishing of Polish Vodka

In Poland things were a little different. Vodka production was assisted in 1546, when King Jan Olbracht passed a law allowing all Poles to produce and sell alcohol. By 1550 there were many production facilities in Cracow, Gdansk, and Poznan, and production and consumption were both on the increase. That all ended, however, in 1572, when the king reassessed the situation and gave exclusive rights of production to the gentry, also requiring them to pay the heavy taxes which came with the privilege.

From the sixteenth ventury onward, vodka production flourished in both countries. As potatoes were gradually introduced to Europe from America, this provided another raw material for vodka production. Potatoes were apparently introduced to Poland in the seventeenth century and used to make vodka by the late eighteenth century. The establishment of many of the distilleries in Poland during the late 1700s (Lvov in 1782 and Lancut in 1784), showed the rise of vodka in all of its different styles. The Lvov distillery (Lvov is now Lviw, in Ukraine), produced 123 different styles of vodkas, along with liqueurs, rums, and araks, and exported products to more than 20 overseas markets.

The country of Poland ceased to exist in 1772, after it was partitioned by Russia, Prussia, and Austria-Hungary.

During the 150 years of partition, the flavored and specialty vodkas were developed into a large number of differing styles, from Zubrowka to Krupnik, Wisniowka to Gnesnania Boonekamp. Even an aged vodka, which still lives as the brand name 'Starka' was developed. This product arose from the custom of filling a used oak wine cask with vodka at the birth of a daughter, and putting it away until her wedding when the vodka was used to toast the health of the bride and groom.

Of the 25 current polmos distilleries in Poland, a number of them were established in the nineteenth Century, including Starogard-Gdansk in 1846, the city where Poland's first rectification plant was established in 1871. Others were the Hartwig-Kantorowicz plant in Poznan and J. Fuchs's distillery in Warsaw, both in 1856, with M. Patsche in 1873 in Warsaw and the Warsaw Rectification Co. in 1889, Bielsko-Biala in 1827, Zielona Gora in 1860, and Siedlce in 1896.

After Poland again fell under the sway of Russia following World War II and the forced installation of Communism, all of the distilleries were combined into the governmental production arm called 'Polmos'. This group, along with the export and marketing branch, Agros, now Agros Trading Ltd., produced and sold all of the vodka in Poland, until the fall of Communism in 1988.

The Smirnoffs in Exile

When Vodka production was banned in the Soviet Union in 1917, many of the families who had produced vodka fled the country and tried to start production in other areas in Europe. The most famous of these families was the Smirnoffs. Before the revolution, they had become wealthy and influential producing vodka. The Smirnoffs owned and controlled the largest distillery in Moscow, which after the revolution was converted into a garage by the Bolsheviks. They had also been the official purveyors of vodka to the tsar's court.

After having fled the new regime, the family started a number of companies, one in Istanbul, another in Lvov, Poland, and a third in France. The French company went bankrupt in 1928, and was sold to one A. Moussatoff who leased the rights to L. Ter-Asarieff, who ran the company in France from 1929 until 1954, when it was sold to Heublein in the U.S.

On another track however, Rudolf Kunett, a native Russian who had emigrated to the U.S., went to France in 1933 where he met with Vladimir Smirnoff, then the managing director of the Smirnoff spirits company. The French company granted Kunett the exclusive rights and licenses on the North American continent to all the products and beverages of the firm. Kunett set up a plant in Bethel, Connecticut, in 1934 and began manufacturing and marketing vodka and other spirits. But he couldn't get vodka to sell, and sold the Smirnoff plant to the Englishman John Martin, chairman of Heublein's. Martin had just as little success at first, but a few years later came up with the idea of 'the Moscow Mule'.

Communist Vodka Policy

In the U.S.S.R., vodka production and sale were prohibited until 1936, when they was restarted on a small scale. From that date until the beginning of the Second World War in 1941, production was still very low and few people drank to excess. It has been claimed that the problem of excessive consumption returned when certain elements of the Stalin government sought to change the social patterns of the people. Some of Stalin's apparatchiks in the law enforcement, justice, and secret police departments hoped to change the attitudes of the people from the strict social mores instituted by the Leninists before Stalin came to power. During the second world war vodka was distributed to the troops with the idea of creating a new group who regarded vodka as a right and consumed it frequently. Excessive consumption of alcohol increasingly became a problem after the war, and the Soviet authorities tried various means to combat it. The last time was under Gorbachev, when official vodka product was sharply cut. There was an immediate increase in illegally-produced vodka, and a sudden shortage of sugar, as millions of Russians diverted all the sugar they could find to the production of bootleg vodka.

Vodka Comes to America

Prior to the beginning of production by Smirnoff in this country, vodka was unknown in the United States. One story tells how a sharp South Carolina salesman, Ed Wooten, introduced the new product in a very unusual manner.

After the purchase of Smirnoff by the Heublein Company, Heublein wanted to move the production facilities from Bethel, Connecticut, to their main plant location in Hartford. So they ordered a manufacturing run of two thousand cases to be prepared for the time period the plant was out of production during the move. Since the order was unexpected, the plant ran out of corks for vodka, and instead used corks printed with the name Smirnoff Whiskey, which the company had also been making and marketing on a test basis.

When the distributor in South Carolina received 25 cases of the new product, Mr. Wooten opened one of the bottles. Upon pulling the cork he saw the name 'Smirnoff Whiskey' printed on the cork and started advertising the product in his area as 'Smirnoff's White Whiskey, No Taste, No Smell.' The idea struck a chord with the consumers in the area, some of whom apparently didn't like the powerful flavor of bourbon. When people discovered that this new spirit mixed with almost anything, sales began growing and Smirnoff was established as a viable brand. If this tale is true, it might seem to indicate that there has always been a hidden demand for the pure, clean taste of vodka.

During World War II, all salable alcohol production was stopped and Smirnoff was put on hold until the war was over. In 1945, the company started up where it had left off. Since then, vodka has gone from a little-known

American drink to the biggest-selling category of distilled spirits, and has largely supplanted gin as a cocktail base.

Vodka sales increased dramatically during the early 1950s, due to innovative advertising aimed at promoting cocktails based on vodka: the first big success was the 'Moscow Mule'. The 'screwdriver' was supposedly invented by American petroleum engineers in the middle east who stirred the vodka and orange juice mixture with screwdrivers. The 'Bloody Mary' began life as the 'Bucket of Blood', created by Fernand Petiot at Harry's New York bar in Paris around 1921. Since he later moved to New York and worked as a bartender at The King Cole Bar of the St. Regis Hotel in Manhattan, this story may have some substance. In New York, he revised the formula, adding spices and Worcestershire sauce, and renamed the drink the 'Red Snapper'. Later again, he changed the name to 'Bloody Mary'. Other popular cocktails were the 'bullshot' (beef bouillon and vodka), and 'Black Russian' (vodka and Kahlúa), developed by regional bartenders but then heavily promoted by the Heublein-owned Smirnoff.

There were few other vodkas available in the U.S., so Smirnoff had the market almost to itself. Its clean, pure taste made it different from what was the primary clear spirit, gin. Smirnoff's sales went from 30,000 cases in 1946 to 273,700 cases in 1951 and up to 418,670 in 1952. The product grew even further to 525,000 cases in 1953. In 1955, it passed the million-case mark, with sales of 1,031,099 and in 1980 passed two million cases. In today's market, while the overall vodka sales level has passed 32 million cases, Smirnoff continues to be the number-one selling vodka brand in the U.S., with 17.6 percent of total sales.

Vodka has recently shared in the general trend of the liquor industry: falling overall sales, but rising sales of the more expensive, high-quality products. There are currently at least a dozen vodkas that call and price themselves as 'premiums' or higher. Many are related to the new growth of the Polish private labels that have grown so fast since the fall of Communism in 1989, but the premiums come from every country and the imports are readily accepted as superior to American-made products.

While the overall American vodka market declines slowly, the share of that market held by U.S. vodka producers falls steeply, and imports of high-priced foreign vodkas show a spectacular rise. It looks as if these trends will continue for some years to come.

PART II

The
World
of
Gins

7

What Gin Is and How It's Made

There's something about a Martini,
Ere the dining and dancing begin,
And to tell you the truth,
It is not the vermouth—
I think that perhaps it's the Gin.

Ogden Nash, *A Drink with Something in It*

Gin was invented in 1650, but that early gin was very different from today's spirit of the same name. Gin has changed continuously from that time until the present day. I define today's gin as a flavored alcoholic drink made from a high-proof neutral spirit, the main flavoring ingredient being the oil of the juniper berry. Other natural vegetable product flavoring agents may also be used to add additional complexity, and these do assist in differentiation between brands and types of gin. Gin has therefore become a particular type of flavored vodka.

My definition essentially agrees with that of the Gin and Vodka Association of Great Britain: "a beverage made from neutral alcohol which has been distilled from cereals, natural sugars or other natural carbohydrates, whose flavor comes from patent mixtures of added fruit, herbs and spices which are always dominated by juniper. It is in the same family as Akavit and Mastika and some might say that it is in the same family as flavored vodkas" (from the Association's book, *Gin*).

In the early days of gin there were many different varities, mostly sweetened. Today there are just three broad types: 1. The ubiquitous dry or London Dry gin. Plymouth Dry was once a distinctive type, but is now incorporated in London Dry. 2. German or 'Steinhager' gin, which differs from regular dry gin only in that, by German law, the sole flavoring permitted is juniper. According to German regulations, gin produced in Germany must be made of water, neutral spirit, natural oil of juniper, and nothing else. 3. Genever. In many ways this is the most interesting kind of gin, and is certainly closest to the original gins, but because of its comparative rarity, I leave genever to the end of this chapter, and will now discuss the dry and Steinhager kinds of gins, though much of what I say will apply to the genevers too.

Buy It, Don't Make It

Gin is always made by adding the flavor of various natural herbs and spices to neutral spirit. So the first stage is to distill the netural spirit, the next is to flavor it with herbs and spices.

Even many experts on alcoholic beverages aren't aware that by far the majority of gins of all types are made by companies who purchase neutral spirit from elsewhere. Almost no gin producers distill their own neutral spirit. The underlying reason for this surprising fact appears to be economic: it is cheaper for some plants to specialize in producing neutral spirit for a variety of end-uses, so even a gin manufacturer who also distilled his own neutral spirit would very likely sell some of that neutral spirit for other purposes, and would see no great advantage in making the gin on the same premises.

Even the Dutch genevers are usually made from a neutral spirit called malt liquor, purchased from grain processors who manufacture the spirit from grain or possibly from molasses left over after the sugar conversion from sugar beets. (Holland and Belgium grow large quantities of beets for conversion into table sugar.) A few Dutch companies do make genever from their own malt wine, but most purchase the base spirit from other companies.

In Germany, the government owns the rectification plants and makes all of the neutral grain spirit in that country. It compels all the German spirit manufacturers to buy the neutral grain spirit from government distilleries, prior to modifying it into whatever product they desire.

In the United Kingdom, the birthplace and traditional home of dry gin, the law actually forbids the making of gin on the same premises that produce neutral grain spirits. This makes it even more likely that the gin companies will purchase the base neutral spirit, rather than making it themselves.

In the U.S., only Seagram's currently has the ability to make its own gin from spirit that it produces itself. Bacardi has the potential to develop that ability, but has just purchased the rights to Bombay Dry and Bombay Sapphire, so will probably not develop a new gin of its own. Midwest Grain does make a gin using base spirit it has produced itself, but this product is sold to and marketed by McCormick Distilling Co. of Weston, Missouri. McCormick was originally the marketing arm of Midwest Grain, but was spun off and sold to former employees during the late 1980s.

All other American gins of which I am aware are made from purchased spirit, always from one of the Big Four: Archer Daniels Midland, Grain Processing, Midwest Grain, or Seagram's. There are currently around 70 different labels of domestically produced gins, mainly made by rectifiers in different regions of the United States. Because of shipping costs, these products are normally sold only in the parts of the country in which they are produced.

Only the major producers like Seagram's, UDV/Diageo, or Barton Brands of Chicago will normally market their brands on a national basis. But many of the most nationally known labels are licensed for manufacture by different rectifiers in different areas of the country.

As far as I have been able to determine, all American gins are made from purchased neutral spirits. None of the U.S. brands even claims that they make the product from scratch, and since only Seagram's has the capability of doing so, I feel fairly safe in stating that all U.S. gins, with the above possible exception, are, like gins all over the world, made from purchased neutral spirit.

Three Ways of Making Gin

Gin can be made in a number of different ways, but there are three main methods used to impart the flavors and aromas of the botanicals—the fruits, herbs, and spices. The three methods are known as *the cold compounding, essential oils,* and *gin head* distillation techniques. Don't confuse these three methods of gin manufacture with the three broad types of gin mentioned above!

Now, just to confuse you further, within the general method known as 'cold compounding', there are in turn three subdivisions—three more narrowly defined techniques.

1. The first type of cold compounding is to precisely measure predetermined amounts of spices and botanicals and to crush these components to assist in the release of the flavors and aromatic portions of these vegetable materials. Then place the botanicals in a predetermined quantity of alcoholic spirit. Leaving the botanicals in the alcohol for the proper predetermined time period means that the full transfer of the necessary tastes and smells to the gin will be ensured. This will usually take about a week, and a further week to allow the spirit to rest and the flavors and aromas to become harmonious. The product is then filtered, diluted to bottle strength, before being bottled and shipped.

2. The second 'cold compounding' technique is to crush the proper amount of botanicals to suit the indi-

vidual gin recipe, place them in a fine mesh cloth bag and submerge the bag and enclosed materials in the proper quantity of alcohol until the flavors and aromas have been transmitted to the alcohol. The bag and botanicals are then removed and the product is allowed to rest for a further time, diluted to bottle strength, bottled, labeled, and shipped.

3. The third 'cold compounding' approach is the circulatory method. Of the three cold compounding methods, it's the least commonly used for making gin, but it is often employed in making cordials or liqueurs. The alcohol is stored in a large tank, and a fine mesh metal tray is suspended above the liquid. The crushed botanicals are placed in the tray and the alcohol is continuously pumped over the botanicals until all the requisite flavors and aromas have been transmitted to the alcohol, thereby making the product into gin. The gin is then allowed to rest for about a week, filtered, and diluted to bottle strength.

In the 'essential oils' method, the neutral grain spirit is contained in a large tank. The botanicals are crushed and cooked in order to remove all of the necessary oils and components from their natural matrix and these are then combined and concentrated into a clear liquid with alcohol which contains all of the flavors and aromas which need to be imparted to the Gin. A measured amount of these essential oils are then added to the main tank of neutral spirit and agitated for a period of time to mix the spirit and flavors and to allow them to merge and marry together. After a week's rest, the product is filtered and diluted to bottle strength.

Finally, in the 'gin head distillation' method, a pot still is used to redistill neutral grain spirit which has been diluted with water, so that the alcohol steam moves past a series of fine mesh metal trays suspended in the neck of the still. The trays are removed and cleaned after each use and new botanicals are crushed and placed in the tray. As the temperature is raised inside the still, the alcohol vaporizes and rises up through the metal tray and the suspended botanicals, thereby imparting the necessary flavors and aromas to the steam, which when condensed becomes the finished product. Since no solid material can pass through the distillation process, no filtration is needed if the gin is made using this method. After the product is condensed, cooled and rested, it is again diluted to bottle strength.

The original and most expensive way is gin-head distillation. Supposedly, only gin-head distilled gins may use the term 'distilled' on the label. The essential oils method was mainly popular during the era of prohibition, since it was the technique used to produce the popular 'bathtub gin', served in speakeasies during that period. But this method is still used to make certain labels. Cold compounding is generally utilized for the mass-produced gins that you will most frequently encounter on the shelves of your liquor or grocery store.

Botanicals and Gin Flavors

Many different vegetable materials, known as 'botanicals', are used to flavor today's gins. These agents include berries, barks, seeds, peels, spices, and roots, which have been in the pharmacopoeia of the alchemist and apothecary since the Middle Ages. Leaves and other materials are sometimes employed for flavoring other types of spirits, but are not normally used in the manufacture of gin.

Juniper berries, which impart a piney taste and smell to the product, are always the source of the predominant flavoring ingredient in gin, and in the case of the German product, Steinhager Dry Gin, the only additive.

The second most commonly used botanical is coriander seed. Many other botanicals may be added according to the individual recipe that each company has devised as its own. Most recipes will include from four to ten of the standard ingredients of aniseed, caraway, and fennel seed, lemon and orange peel (from both bitter and sweet oranges), cassia bark, cumin and cinnamon, licorice and violet root, angelica and orris root, ginger and cardamom, cubeb berries, almonds or almond powder, savory, and nutmeg.

These are the main sources of the flavors and aromas used to make today's dry gins. Other natural flavoring substances, running into the hundreds, are occasionally used for gin but more frequently for cordials and liqueurs. Different gins use different combinations of botanicals, so almost every gin has a unique flavor, however similar all gins may seem to the novice. A new gin label will sometimes represent an attempt to try a different combination of botanicals, to see whether the public will go for this new combination of flavors.

Here's a simple recipe utilized for making a basic gin. To 2,000 liters of 100 proof alcohol, add 45.4 kilograms (100 pounds) of juniper berries, 22.7 kilograms (50 pounds) of coriander seeds, 4.5 kilograms (10 pounds) of cinnamon bark, 4.5 kilograms (10 pounds) of angelica root, 0.45 kilograms (1 pound) of lemon peel, and .45 kilograms (1 pound) of cardamom. The end result will be immediately recognizable as gin.

Each individual herb, spice or other botanical can be used to add different factors to the overall taste and feel of the final spirit. The aim is to give each label its own recognizable character. Currently, however, the trend seems to be for the 'lighter' end of the gin spectrum, in other words, for a gin with fewer botanicals in lower concentrations—another confirmation that modern gin is basically a form of vodka. This trend does give us an easy way to classify gin flavors: the more traditional gins are basically more heavily flavored with juniper and other botanicals, the lighter gins less so.

Of the more traditional or heavily junipered spirits, 'Plymouth' and 'Tanqueray' are probably the most well-known. Of the lighter styles, Bombay Sapphire is currently the booming rage with the newly introduced Leyden gin also vying for attention.

But as to the use of those flavoring and aromatic agents that are called botanicals. Below is the list of fruits, herbs and spices primarily used to impart the flavors which produce gin.

The Most Common Gin Botanicals

Angelica

This is an aromatic root normally found in the northern areas of France, Belgium, and Germany, and occasionally in southern Norway. It is used as a fixative for the flavors and aromas imparted by the other botanicals.

Aniseed

Aniseed is the fragrant seed of the anise plant (*Pimpinella anisum*), which has been used for centuries as a spice for cooking and as a medicinal herb. It is a small plant found in North Africa and Southern Europe which tastes like licorice candy. It is also used to flavor beverages other than gin, such as Anisette and Campari. The related star anise is employed for such spirits as Sambuca

Cassia

Cassia (Chinese cinnamon) is derived from any number of shrubs or trees belonging to the Senna family. It is used as a flavoring agent, though the pulp of the seed pods is useful as a laxative. Primarily the dried buds are employed.

Calamus

An aromatic herb from Asia, calamus may be taken from a climbing palm tree. It was known to the ancient Greek physician Hippocrates as a digestive tonic.

Caraway

This is a biennial European plant, a member of the parsley family. Its fruits are small, spicy, aromatic seeds, widely used in cooking and flavoring. These seeds have been found in archeological digs in Switzerland where they were dated as early as 6000 B.C.

Cardamoms

These are seeds taken from plants, members of the ginger family, which grow in India and China. Cardamoms are the third most expensive spice in the world after vanilla and saffron.

Cinnamon

Cinnamon is the spice we all know which adds heat and flavor to almost everything. It comes from the inner bark of a number of varieties of the laurel tree, and in the preparation of gin is mainly used as an undertone.

Coriander

Coriander is a parsley-like plant (the fresh leaves are familiar as cilantro) whose pungent, strong-smelling seeds have longitudinal ridges. It's one of the oldest known spices, and has long been considered a medicinal herb which can strengthen the wind or breath by its beneficial effect upon the lungs and respiratory system.

Cubeb

These berries are the fruits of a shrub, a member of the pepper family usually grown in Eastern India. They have been used for centuries as an herb for the treatment of urinary problems and bronchial ailments. In the last century and even continuing in some quarters as late as the 1940s, they were smoked in the form of cigarettes.

Cumin

This spice is an annual of the carrot family with fennel-like leaves. It is used mainly in cooking and in Eastern countries as a condiment. It's also a vital ingredient in the favorite dish of the southwestern United States—chili.

Fennel

Fennel is a tall stout herb of the parsley family with yellow flowers whose seeds are highly pungent and used in many cooking sauces. It serves as an aromatic fixative when used in gin. The plant can grow quite large, sometimes reaching 15 feet in height. It is cultivated in the U.S. as an herb for its seeds, and to use as a spice in cooking.

Ginger

The spice ginger comes from a root structure, or rhizome, of the ginger plant. It's very commonly used in cooking and is regarded as a general tonic.

Grains of Paradise

These are intensely peppery berries from West Africa. The seeds of a plant (*Aframomum Melegueta*) which is a member of the ginger family, they can be used to intensify the flavoring effects of all the other botanicals in gin.

Juniper

These berries are small, hard, and purplish-colored. The use of these berries, or the oil pressed from them, imparts a piney, evergreen odor and taste; the smell sometimes even begins to hint at turpentine. The juniper bush is indeed a member of the pine family and has been known for centuries as a strong diuretic which has the effect of cleaning out the kidneys.

Lemon

The peel of this fruit is used to impart the citrus astringency which gives gin its clean, dry nose and taste. Since only the zest or colored portion of the peel is used as a gin flavoring agent, only the oil from the peel is actually transferred. The best lemons are grown in Italy and Spain.

Licorice

Licorice is the root of a perennial herb found in central and southern Europe. It's used in both medicine and candy-making, and imparts the well-known piquant flavor, very similar to that which can also be obtained from aniseed.

Nutmeg

Nutmeg is an aromatic kernel of the fruit of various tropical trees (genus *Myristica*), especially those of the nutmeg tree, which imparts a musky flavor and aroma to gin.

Orange

The peel of both bitter and sweet organges is used, bitter to lend astringency in a manner similar to lemons, and sweet to give an impression of sweetness. Since only the zest or colored part of the peel is used, there is no transference of true sugars, only the 'impression' of these.

Orris

Orris is the root of the Florentine iris. It's cultivated in the south of France and Italy, and serves as a flavor fixative. It is also used as an aromatic fixative for perfumes.

Rosemary

The leaves are used as a spice and come from the rosemary plant, an evergreen fragrant shrub (*Rosmarinus officinalis*) of the mint family. This plant grows in southern Europe and western Asia and usually has small blue flowers. It has traditionally been cultivated for its stimulating and refreshing aromas.

Savory

Savory is a hardy, annual, aromatic herb of the mint family, used to bring out the flavors of the other herbs.

Genevers

Genevers have been made in Holland (the Netherlands) since gin was invented there in the mid-seventeenth century. There are currently 32 distilleries in The Netherlands (see Appendix C), and all of them produce genevers. Other styles of gins can also be made by these distilleries. At least one dry gin, 'Leyden', is made in Holland, at the Dirkswager distillery in Schiedam.

Genevers are the gins that adhere most closely to the original gins first produced by Dr. Sylvius. They are produced from a malty spirit (called malt liquor) and usually will have a strong presence of malt mingled with the juniper flavor and aroma. Genevers come in three different age classifications, 'jonge', an unaged spirit; 'oude', stored at least one year in small oak barrels, and so I am told, a medium aged spirit which I have not yet seen or sampled.

Genevers are still sold around the world and would most often be drunk neat or over ice, because the taste of the malt conflicts with most standard mixers. However, some of these products are today light enough that they can make acceptable martinis. I always recommend experimenting with new tastes.

Some of these products have been around for two or three hundred years. The Bols company has been in existence since 1575 and has been making genever since shortly after its development in 1650.

The formula for genever has been adapted since that time to keep pace with the changing drinking habits and styles of the world, but the techniques of manufacture and the aromatics employed to make genevers have remained remarkably constant for the last 300 years or so.

8
Gins of Europe and America

Of all the gin joints in all the towns in all the world, she walks into mine.

Richard Blaine in Julius J. Epstein et al., *Casablanca*

This chapter surveys all gins under three headings: American, imported, and genevers. Of course, genevers are all imported, but they are so remarkable, and so historically interesting, that they deserve separate treatment.

American Gins

Ancient Age Gin

This product may have been a close-out, since I saw it being sold at a very inexpensive price in a warehouse-style liquor store. It's apparently made by the Ancient Age Spirits Co. in their Leestown Distillery in Frankfort, Kentucky, which is best known for its Ancient Age Bourbon. This product is owned and distributed by the Sazerac Company of New Orleans.

Aristocrat Gin

This 11th best-selling gin is made and marketed by Heaven Hill Distilleries along with their 'Burnett's White Satin Gin', the fifth best-selling gin in the U.S.

Banker's Club Gin

This label is manufactured and marketed by Laird's & Co. a family-run corporation best-known for their apple-jack (apple brandy). They also make and market four other gin labels: 'Five O'clock Distilled Extra Dry', 'Kasser's 51 London Dry', 'Laird's Extra Dry London Dry', and 'Senator's Club Extra Dry Distilled London Dry'.

Barclay's London Dry Gin

Manufactured and marketed by Barton Brands Ltd., a major liquor distributor based in Chicago. This company also makes nine other gin labels: 'Barton Extra', 'Crystal Palace', 'Fleischmann's', 'Glenmore London Extra Dry', 'Mr. Boston's English Market Dry', 'Mr. Boston's Riva London Dry', 'Pikeman Premium London Dry', 'Schenley London Dry', and 'Skol'.

Barrett's Gin

Manufactured and marketed by Frank-Lin Distiller's Products Co. regional manufacturer and distributor. This company also makes or markets six other gins: 'Bellringer 94.4° Premium Imported', 'Crown Russe', 'Cossack', 'Glenwood', 'Martini 90°', and 'Potter's'.

Barton's Extra Dry Gin

Manufactured and marketed by Chicago-based Barton Brands. This company makes nine other gins: 'Barclay's', 'Crystal Palace', 'Fleischmann's', 'Glenmore London Extra Dry', 'Mr. Boston's English Market Dry', 'Mr. Boston's Riva London Dry Gin', 'Pikeman Premium London Dry', 'Schenley London Dry', and 'Skol'.

Bentley's Extra Dry Distilled London Dry Gin

Manufactured and marketed by Majestic Distilling Company of Baltimore, Maryland. This East coast regional label is joined by 'Black Watch Dry Gin', 'Classic Club London Dry Gin', 'Club 400 Distilled Dry Gin', 'Lord Baltimore Dry Gin', 'Odesse Gin', 'Rikaloff Dry Gin', and 'Traveler's Club Extra Dry Gin', all from the same company.

Black Watch Distilled London Dry Gin

Manufactured and marketed by Majestic, this is a regional label on the East coast and is joined by a number of other labels which include 'Bentley's Extra Dry Gin', 'Classic Club Gin', 'Club 400 Distilled Dry Gin', 'Lord Baltimore London Dry Gin', 'Odesse Gin', 'Rikaloff Distilled Dry Gin', and 'Traveler's Club Extra Dry Gin', all from the same company.

Booth's London Dry Gin

Founded in the 1700s, this long-standing brand is currently manufactured and marketed in the U.S. by the UDV/Diageo mega-conglomerate, which also makes Gordon's London Dry Gin in their distillery in Plainfield, Illinois. Both of these products are made in the old way of redistilling neutral spirit in a 'gin head', with racks in the neck of the still holding the botanicals.

One of the two brothers who founded the company, Felix, was very well-educated and received a baronetcy from William IV in 1835. He died in 1850 and the title and company passed to his nephew, Williamson Booth, a bachelor like his uncle before him. His death caused the passage to his brother Charles, another bachelor; upon his death in 1896, the baronetcy became extinct and 'Booth's' became a limited company.

Boord's London Dry Gin

Made by different companies under license, it is one of the many products manufactured and marketed on the West Coast by Frank-Lin.

Burnett's London Dry Gin

The company has records that show production since 1679 in England, but it is now an American gin, manufactured and marketed by the Heaven Hill Company of Bardstown, Kentucky who also makes 'Aristocrat' gin.

Sir Robert Burnett joined the company in 1770 and began a career that spiraled upward at an ever-increasing pace. He was named Lord Mayor of London in 1794 and knighted the following year.

Calvert London Dry Gin

This label, the #13 leading brand with 1997 sales of 82,000 cases, is manufactured and marketed by Jim Beam Brands, which also owns and markets one other gin label, Gilbey's.

Cascade Mountain Gin

Manufactured and marketed by a very small company, Bendistillery Co. of Bend, Oregon. This company uses juniper berries from the state of Washington; the finished product is available only in the state of Oregon. The company is owned and run by the Bendis family, who claim to use a very small copper pot still to distill their gin.

Classic Club Distilled London Dry Gin

Manufactured and marketed by Majestic Distilling Company, this East coast regional spirit is joined by the labels 'Bentley's', 'Black Watch', 'Club 400', 'Odesse', 'Rikaloff', and 'Traveler's Club', all from the same company.

Club 400 Distilled Dry Gin

Manufactured and marketed by Majestic Distilling Company of Baltimore, Maryland. This East coast regional brand is joined by the labels 'Bentley's', 'Black Watch', 'Classic Club', 'Lord Baltimore', 'Odesse', 'Rikaloff', and 'Traveler's Club'.

Cossack Gin

This brand is currently produced in the U.S. by Frank-Lin Distillers Products Co.. The same trademark is used in the United Kingdom by United Distillers of London, England; I am unaware whether there is a licensing agreement between these two companies. Frank-Lin also produces and markets five other domestic gins: 'Barrett's', 'Crown Russe', 'Glenwood', 'Martini 90°', and 'Potter's'.

Crown Russe Gin

Manufactured and marketed by Frank-Lin. This company also makes and markets five other gins: 'Barrett's', 'Cossack', 'Glenwood', 'Martini 90°', and 'Potter's'.

Crystal Palace Gin

This is one of the ten gins manufactured and marketed by Barton Brands. The others are 'Barclay's London Dry', 'Barton Extra Dry', 'Crystal Palace', 'Fleischmann's', 'Glenmore London Extra Dry', 'Mr. Boston's English Market Dry', 'Mr. Boston's Riva London Dry', 'Pikeman Premium London Dry', 'Schenley London Dry', and 'Skol'.

English Guard London Dry Gin

This gin is made and marketed by United States Distilled Products Co. of St. Paul, Minnesota. A sister label is Hayes and Hunnicutt gin.

Five O'clock Distilled Extra Dry Gin

This is one of the five brands manufactured and marketed by Laird & Co., the others are 'Banker's Club', 'Kasser's 51 London Dry', 'Laird's Extra Dry London Dry', and 'Senator's Club Extra Dry Distilled London Dry'. All are made by the standard method of purchasing neutral grain spirit and performing the proprietary modifications to turn it into gin.

Fleischmann's Gin

One of the ten standard gins manufactured and marketed by Barton Brands Ltd.

Gilbey's Distilled London Dry Gin

Founded by two brothers, Walter and Alfred Gilbey, after they returned from the Crimean War, the company first started as a wine brokerage in 1857. The business grew to the point where they needed to start their own distillery, which they did in 1872. In 1962, the English company merged with United Wine Traders to become IDV, the spirits arm of Grand Metropolitan.

Gilbey's is now the #3-selling brand in the U.S. with 1997 sales of 721,000 nine-liter cases. It's manufactured and marketed by Jim Beam Brands, which purchased the U.S. rights through a license granted in 1938.

Glenmore London Extra Dry Gin

One of the ten standard brands manufactured and marketed by Barton Brands Ltd.

Glenwood Gin

A regional brand normally found only on the West Coast, this gin is manufactured and marketed by Frank-Lin Distiller's Products Ltd. The other brands of this company are 'Barrett's', 'Crown Russe', 'Cossack', 'Martini 90°', and 'Potter's'.

Gordon's Distilled London Dry Gin

Founded in 1769 by Alexander Gordon, who was succeeded by his son and he by his grandson. In 1877 Charles Gordon sold the company distillery to John Currie & Co. and began making the gin with purchased spirit. In 1898, Gordon's merged with Charles Tanqueray & Co. to form the largest gin company in the world at that time.

Today the domestic product is manufactured at the UDV/Diageo plant in Plainfield, Illinois, and is the #2 selling brand with 1997 sales of 1,115,000 cases. The product has been made under license in the U.S. since the 1930s and is made in the same plant as Booth's. The gin itself is made by the original 'gin head' method (see Chapter 7), with the original botanical recipe.

Hayes and Hunnicutt Gin

This domestic gin is manufactured and marketed by United States Distilled Products Co. A sister label is 'English Guard London Dry'.

Kasser's 51 London Dry Gin

Manufactured and marketed by Laird & Co. as one of their five labels of gins and vodkas, this is a standard gin.

Kavlana Gin

One of the brands manufactured and marketed on the West Coast by Frank-Lin.

Laird's Extra Dry Distilled London Dry Gin

One of the five gins made and marketed by Laird & Co. this gin is a standard production gin which does have some national distribution.

Llord's Gin

Where it comes from I don't know. The company given on the label no longer has a listed telephone number.

Lord Baltimore Gin

Manufactured and marketed by Majestic Distilling Company, this East Coast regional label is joined by 'Bentley's', 'Black Watch', 'Classic Club', 'Club 400', 'Odesse', 'Rikaloff', and 'Traveler's Club', all made as standard gins.

Martini 90° Gin

This gin is produced and promoted by Frank-Lin and is available chiefly on the West coast.

McColl's Gin

A regional gin manufactured and marketed by Montebello Brands Co. of Baltimore. This is a standard gin, available mainly in the Northeast region of the U.S.

McCormick Distilled London Dry Gin

This standard production gin, a surprisingly good gin for the money, is made by the original 'gin head' method by Midwest Grain Co. for McCormick Distilling Co. The latter firm was originally the marketing branch of Midwest Grain, but is now a separate company.

Monogram Diluted Gin

Manufactured and marketed by Frank-Lin, this regional product is available mainly in California.

Mr. Boston's English Market Gin

This is one of the ten standard gins manufactured and marketed by Barton Brands of Chicago.

Mr. Boston's Riva London Dry Gin

Another standard gin produced and marketed by Barton Brands Ltd.

Odesse Gin

An East Coast regional spirit, manufactured and marketed by Majestic.

Paramount Gin

Manufactured and marketed by Paramount Distillers Inc. of Cleveland, Ohio, this standard regional gin is mainly available only in Ohio.

Pikeman Premium London Dry Gin

One of the ten gins manufactured and marketed by Barton Brands.

Popov Gin

Manufactured and marketed by Heublein Inc., a wholly owned subsidiary of UDV/Diageo, this variant is an off-shoot of Popov vodka, the lower-priced alternative to Smirnoff, also produced by Heublein.

Potter's Gin

This standard gin is made under license by Frank-Lin and is one of their six gins.

Rikaloff Gin

One of ten standard gins manufactured and marketed by Majestic.

Schenley London Dry Gin

This standard production gin is one of ten produced by Barton Brands.

Seagram's Extra Dry Gin

This gin is produced at the Seagram's distillery in Lawrenceburg, Indiana, by their own proprietary methods. They do make their own neutral grain spirit, however, their plant being one of the Big Four grain processors. This 'gin head–distilled' gin (see Chapter 7) was introduced in 1939 and since then has been one of the leading domestic gins available.

Seagram's Excel Premium Extra Dry Gin

This premium gin is made by Seagram's at their Lawrenceburg, Indiana distillery. I have not been able to ascertain what process they use to make this gin better than their regular gin, but it certainly has a distinctive appeal.

Seagram's Lime Twisted Gin

This gin is apparently the same as their regular gin but with more lime zest added. It makes a very decent gin and tonic.

Senator's Club Extra Dry London Dry Gin

This standard production gin is manufactured and marketed by Laird & Co., who produce four other gins in their New Jersey plant for distribution mainly in the Eastern U.S. The other four are 'Banker's Club', 'Five O'clock Distilled Extra Dry', 'Kasser's 51 London Extra Dry', and 'Laird's Extra Dry Distilled London Dry'.

Skol Gin

One of the ten gins made by Barton Brands.

Traveler's Club Extra Dry Gin

One of eight standard gins made by Majestic Distilling of Baltimore.

Imported Gins

Beefeater London Distilled Dry Gin

Founded in 1863 when James Burroughs bought John Taylor & Son, rectifiers of liqueurs and gin. Upon his death in 1897, the company passed to his two oldest sons, Fred and Ernest, who were later joined by the youngest, Frank. In 1908, Burrough's moved their location from Chelsea to Lambeth, where production is still located. The company continued to be family owned and operated until 1987, when it was purchased by Whitbread. In 1991 the company became part of Allied Lyons, today Allied-Domecq.

Searching for a name for his new gin, Mr. Burroughs looked no further than the Tower of London, a few miles from the distillery. He picked the 'Yeoman Warder' guards of the Tower as his symbol and the namesake of the brand. These men were given a very large portion of beef at their evening meals to make them strong, so that they became known as 'Beef-eaters'.

Beefeater is a cold-compounded or steeped gin in which the botanicals are allowed to steep in the alcohol for 24 hours before being redistilled, filtered, diluted, and bottled. It is currently the #2-selling imported gin in the U.S. with 1997 sales of 640,000 cases.

Bellringer 94.4° Premium

A British gin imported by Frank-Lin, it is marketed mainly on the West Coast.

Bombardier Dry Gin

This gin is imported by Gil Schy and Co. of upstate New York. I have been unable to contact this firm, so the product may be leftover stock and the company out of business.

Bombay Dry Gin

Famous for many years, this traditional English gin is imported and marketed by Barcardi-Martini USA, but is now being overshadowed by its stablemate, Bombay Sapphire. It is a classic distilled dry gin with the purchased spirit being redistilled in a pot with the alcohol vapors passing through racks suspended in the neck of the still containing the botanicals. The botanicals used in Bombay Dry are; juniper berries and orris root (iris) from Italy, coriander seeds from Morocco, angelica root from Saxony, Cassia bark from Indochina, almonds and lemon peel from Spain and licorice from China. Now the #4-selling imported gin is the U.S., 1997 sales were 165,000 nine-liter cases.

Bombay Sapphire Distilled London Dry Gin

This fastest-growing example of the rebirth of the imported gins is made in England from meticulously selected ingredients. Using an original process that employs the only four Carterhead stills in the world, this gin strives to be recognized as the very best. (Carterhead stills are a special model combining features of the pot still and the column still.) The company uses ten botanicals in their process, in which the grain alcohol is redistilled and the vapors are passed over the botanicals in a separate basket before being condensed and diluted to bottle strength. They are proud of their use of the highest quality botanicals, so that they provide a list of these aromatic taste altering substances. The botanicals are: juniper berries and orris root from Italy, coriander seeds from Morocco, almonds and lemon peel from Spain, licorice and cassia bark from China, angelica root from Saxony, cubeb berries from Java and, grains of paradise from West Africa. All these ingredients are crushed, grated or ground up to release the most flavor and are then packed into the baskets in the distillation units. After the distillation and condensation of the resulting flavored liquid, the spirit is filtered, diluted with the purest water and bottled.

This fastest-growing product in the imported gin category was #3 in sales for 1997 with 250,000 cases.

Boodle's British Gin London Dry Gin

This premium imported gin was created in 1847 and is named after the Boodle's Club in London. It is the only gin in the U.K. that is produced in a vacuum still, allowing distillation at lower temperatures to lock in the botanical flavors. The botanicals beside juniper berries include: coriander, sage, cassia bark, nutmeg, rosemary, caraway, and angelica root. This combination of botanicals gives Boodle's an immediately distinctive flavor.

Bradburn's English Gin

This import claims to distill the botanicals in a sequential order to produce a supremely smooth gin. It may be a close-out, since it was purchased for a very low price in a large warehouse-style liquor store. So it may no longer be being imported by Paddington Corporation, a subsidiary of UDV/Diageo.

Citadelle Gin

This 1999 release from France is definitely a new taste in the market. Made with 19 different botanicals, the gin is dry, yet very floral in all of its accents. Imported by Integrity Wine and Spirits of Newport Beach, California, this gin is made by the Gabriel and Andreu distillery just outside Cognac, France. It's a sister to the vodka 'French Alps', made in the same distillery and imported by the same company.

Cork Dry Gin

This Irish gin is triple-distilled from grain by the master distillers at the distillery of Cork Distilleries Company, North Mall, Cork, Ireland. The product is then blended with a complex mix of juniper, citrus, and other botanical flavors to give it a subtle difference of its own. They then add something called a 'Watercourse Note', that is the dry trademark of Cork's historic Watercourse Distillery. It is imported into the U.S. by Austin-Nichols, a division of Pernod-Ricard of France. Huzzar vodka is made at the same location.

Corney & Barrows London Distilled Dry Gin

The company was founded in 1780 when Edward Bland Corney opened a small wine shop on Broad Street in London. When he died in 1833, his son, Thomas, took over the business. In 1838, a cousin, Robert Phillipson Barrow was brought into the business as a partner and the name was changed to its current incarnation. This gin is considered to be among the best made in England.

Horse Guard London Dry Gin

Manufactured at the Loch Lomond distillery in Scotland, owned by the Glen Catrine Bonded Warehouse, a privately-held family business that produces many malt whiskys, this gin is currently being imported by Preiss Imports of Los Angeles.

Leyden Dry Gin

This fine gin is distilled and bottled at the Dirkswager distillery in Schiedam, Holland, one of only four plants left in the city which once had over 50 distilleries. Schiedam was a major grain port during the seventeeth, eighteenth, and nineteenth centuries. The distillery currently purchases neutral spirit from one of the grain spirit suppliers in the area, and then re-distills the spirit, adds the botanicals as essences, and lets the product rest and meld together for an additional week or so.

Old Raj Dry Gin

A product of Cadenhead's, made in the Springbank Scotch whisky distillery in Campbeltown. This high (110) proof gin is definitely different from the majority of gins made in the U.K. and is intended primarily as a reincarnation of the older style gins that were used to make gin and tonic in the tropic zones of the old British empire when there was no ice. It's also rather pricey at over $50.00 per bottle, but I think the difference is worth it. It is imported and distributed nationally by Preiss Imports.

Plymouth Gin

Re-introduced after a 20-year absence from the U.S., this classic gin is made at the Black Friars distillery of Coates and Co. in the city of Plymouth, England. This dry gin was begun in the late 1700s and has continued through all of the changes to the industry since then. By its connection to the Royal Navy, this gin has come to be regarded as one of the originators of most of the drinks that use gin. Royal Navy surgeons in the past used Plymouth Gin to encourage the consumption of Angostura bitters or 'pink gins', to combat certain diseases. The first ever publication of a recipe for the classic martini specifies Plymouth Gin plus a dry vermouth and a dash of bitters.

Currently this 82.4 proof version is available in the US through Todhunter Imports, with other versions available in the UK at 96.4 proof and 114 proof. The company has gone through many different owners since the original founding family sold out, but is now back in the hands of small private investors who have hopes of repositioning this fine gin.

Schlichte Steinhager Dry Gin

Dating from the 1766 founding of the Schlichte company, Steinhager gin, by German law, can only be produced from triple distilled grain spirit, juniper berries, and water. Steinhager distillate is reduced to drinking proof by the addition of pure spring water and is bottled in stone crocks to preserve the distinct aroma. Currently imported by Niche Imports of Morris Plains, New Jersey.

Tanqueray Special Dry Distilled English Gin

Founded in 1830 by Charles Tanqueray, the first Tanqueray distillery made many different types of gins. During the 1870s the styles of gins began to change from sweet to dry, and by the turn of the century all gins were being sold as dry gins. The Tanqueray company also introduced stoneware crocks at a time when gins had been sold only in barrels, and this innovation allowed the sale of gin in groceries and wine shops. In 1898 Tanqueray and Gordon's gins merged to form the world's largest gin company at that time.

This fine gin is now the number one seller among imported gins in the U.S., with 1997 sales of 1,355,000 cases; it's imported by Schieffelin & Somerset.

Tanqueray Malacca Gin

This gin uses a different formulation from the original Tanqueray listed above. The main difference is a heavier concentration of cinnamon and more than average amounts of lemon zest and coriander. This creates a highly distinctive taste profile that can make for some interesting flavor differences in your regular mixed drinks.

Genever Gins

Genevers are a staple alcoholic beverage of the many liquor distillers in Holland. Currently there are 32 distilleries in operation in that country, mainly manufacturing genevers and liqueurs. (See Appendix E.) Many of the products called jonge (young) are really vodkas. Vodka under that name does not sell very well in the Netherlands, so as a marketing tool the companies call their pure spirit 'young genever', and it sells very well indeed.

Genevers are gins. They are admittedly very different from the products called dry gins which we mostly consume in the U.S. today, but definitely gins. They're not at all like the English gins, and may take some getting used to, but they have a romantic charm of their own. The 'oude' or old genevers can stand alone as a specific group, with their malty base separating them from the more popular dry gins. They do not generally mix well. But the 'jonge' genevers are very light and dry and can be mixed just as a vodka.

Bokma Genever Gin

Manufactured in Holland by one part of the Bols company, this genever is marketed by Preiss Imports.

Bols Genever Gin

Bols is the oldest liquor company in Holland. Founded in 1575, it actually predates by 75 years Dr. Silvius's invention of gin! This company currently makes and markets all types of spirits, but mainly concentrate on genevers and liqueurs.

Boomsma Jonge Genever Gin

Manufactured by the Boomsma Company in Leeuwarden, this young Genever is imported and marketed in the U.S. by CVI Brands of San Carlos, California. The brand is actually owned by the Bols Benelux Co.

Boomsma Oude Genever Gin

This old genever, manufactured by the Boomsma Company in Leeuwarden, is aged in oak barrels for at least one year and is imported into the U.S. by CVI Brands of San Carlos, California.

De Kuyper Genever Gin

Manufactured in the de Kuyper distillation plant in the town of Schiedam, from purchased malt liquor, which is made from a mixture of malted barley and other grains. Marketed in the U.S. by Jim Beam Brands.

EXTRA DRY

Glenmore®

London Dry
GIN

MADE FROM 100%
GRAIN NEUTRAL SPIRITS
ACCORDING TO A
FAMOUS OLD FORMULA

40% ALC/VOL (80 PROOF)
BOTTLED BY GLENMORE DISTILLE
OWENSBORO, KY-ALBANY, GA

EXTRA DRY QUALITY

BLACK WATCH

DISTILLED
LONDON DRY
GIN

40% ALC. BY VOL.
(80 PROOF)
DISTILLED FROM GRAIN
PRODUCT OF U.S.A.

BOTTLED BY
MONUMENTAL DISTILLING CO.
BALTIMORE, MD.

FLEISCHMANN'S
Established 1870

EXTRA DRY
GIN

100% Neutral Spirits
Distilled from Grain
0% Alc / Vol. (80 Proof)

BOTTLED BY
FLEISCHMANN DISTILLING CO
Owensbo

928 21021   1   1,3

PRODUCT OF U.S.A. · "HIGH & DRY" REGISTERED U.S. PATENT AND TRADEMARK OFFICE

EST. 1740

BOOTH'S

Distilled
London Dry
Gin

100% Neutral Spirits Distilled from Grain

90 PROOF

DISTILLED & BOTTLED BY THE BOOTH'S DISTILLERY (U.S.A.) LINFIELD, R.
UNDER THE SUPERVISION OF BOOTH'S DISTILLERIES LTD. LONDON, ENGLAND

ONE LITRE

EXTRA DRY

Barclay's®

London Dry
Gin

Bottled by
Barton Distilling Company
Bardstown, Ky, Los Angeles, Ca, Atlanta, Ga.
40% ALC./VOL. (80 PROOF) · 100% GRAIN NEUTRAL SPIRITS

PIKEMAN

Premium London Dry
GIN

100% GRAIN NEUTRAL SPIRITS

40% Alc/Vol (80 Proof)

BOTTLED BY BARTON DISTILLING COMPANY
BARDSTOWN, KENTUCKY · LOS ANGELES, CALIFORNIA

9
Gin Tasting Notes

Though I own even then I should see no great sin in it
Were there three drops of Sir Felix's gin in it.

Richard Harris Barham, *The Ingoldsby Legends*

In this chapter I provide tasting notes for regular dry gins, followed by one for a 'flavored gin', and then by a few genevers.

Ancient Age Ultra Smooth Extra Dry Gin, 80 Proof

Clean and bright, medium viscosity, good legs, lemon zest in the nose, with a lighter juniper and more coriander than usual, and light nasal burn. Medium alcohol attack with burn to the front edges and center of the tongue. Fairly harsh bite to the throat and a slightly sweet aftertaste with burn down the throat.

Barton's London Extra Dry Gin, 80 proof

Clear and clean, medium viscosity with good legs. Dry nasal feel with mild alcohol burn and very light juniper with few other aromas. Light mouth feel with mild alcohol burn to the tongue, slightly sweet aftertaste with a medium finish.

Beefeater's London Dry Gin, 94 proof

Clean and clear with a hint of beige, smooth on the glass with long legs. To the nose, good juniper with some citric zest, probably lemon and a solid nasal burn. In the mouth a slight bitterness at first that is overpowered by the alcohol attack over the entire tongue, oily with little chewiness, but a certain tartness, reminiscent of lemon. The aftertaste is lightly tart and piney with a long finish and a little burn to the soft palate.

Bombay Dry Gin, 86 proof

Clear and clean with a light hint of color and some chatoyance, good viscosity with long legs. A light nose with the juniper strangely not as dominant as most, more coriander is present with the possibility of other botanicals overriding the juniper. In the mouth the piney taste of the juniper is more evident, but still is challenged by the other botanicals. The spirit has little burn in the mouth but a light citrus feel and the aftertaste has a certain vegetative taste with a long finish.

Bombay Sapphire London Dry Gin, 94 proof

Clean and clear with no color, and long slender legs. A light nasal burn and light aromas of any kind, with a little juniper, lemon zest, and coriander in the nose. Oily and chewy in the mouth with a strong burn to the tongue and a smooth piney taste to the palate. The aftertaste shows burn to the palate and the tongue which slowly subsides to a smooth sweetness and a long finish. Bombay Saphire is very pleasant, a little lighter in flavor than most, but eminently drinkable.

Boodle's British Gin, 90.4 proof

No hint of color, good legs. Juniper nose with just a hint of cedar. Astringent first sip with some alcohol burn to the center of the tongue. Good flavor of juniper, with a light sting to the back of the throat. Pleasantly herbal aftertaste with a long and smooth, lingering finish. Boodle's has always been one of my personal favorites, and my comprehensive investigation of its many rivals has not lessened my admiration for it.

Bradburn's English Gin, 94.8 proof

Clean and clear, medium viscosity with good legs. First nose gives a minty juniper aroma, something like a bubble gum, with a light alcohol nasal burn. A strong alcohol burn throughout the mouth, from the lips to the palate and makes the tongue feel as if it's peppery hot. The aftertaste is slightly acrid with an acidic burn which turns slightly sweet and finishes with a softening to mellow.

Burnett's London Dry Gin, 80 proof

Clear as water, with good legs left after the gin slides down the side of the glass. Mildly spirity nose, with a light clean juniper aroma and a little alcohol sting to the sinus. A sharp, almost peppery initial impression in the mouth with a stronger juniper flavor than the nose would bring you to expect. A medium burn to the tongue and some burn to the soft palate but not down the throat. The peppery feel lasts through to the aftertaste, with a medium, slightly tart, long finish. A certain crisp, almost astringent feel at the end.

Cadenhead's Old Raj Dry Gin, 110 proof

In the bottle this gin has a very definite pale green tint though it's very clean and clear with long elegant legs and little light refraction. Considering the alcoholic strength of this spirit, there is surprisingly little sinus burn unless you inhale strongly, but the aroma is a little different from most other gins with a hint of mint in the background and less juniper aroma than most though it is well balanced. The first sip reveals a little sweetness with some heat to the tip and center of the tongue and a very faint feel of citrus. The aftertaste remains slightly sweet in tone, with a pleasantly long herbal finish which slows the need for another sip.

Calvert London Dry Gin, 80 proof

Clear as water with long smooth legs leaving little droplets down the side of the glass. Mild alcohol to the nose with a very light feel of juniper and almost no other discernible botanicals in the aroma. Smooth and mild to the palate with little burn mainly concentrated in the center of the tongue and some heat at the top of the throat. A good aftertaste reveals a little more complexity than the nose would lead you to expect, with a medium aftertaste and a smooth, lingering, medium-long finish.

Cascade Mountain Gin, 95 proof

The barest hint of color, with a thicker viscosity and short legs. The aroma of juniper is very light with no trace of other botanicals to the nose and no alcohol sting to the nasal passages. Very smooth in the mouth with again a very light juniper flavor and no other discernible botanicals. Some sting and heat of the alcohol, with the main attack concentrating in the middle of the tongue and continuing to the back of the throat when swallowing. Alcohol heat remains in the mouth for a good duration, there's almost no aftertaste, and the finish slowly cools with an intake of breath.

Cork Dry Gin, 80 proof

Clear and clean with very long legs on the side of the glass. A good dry aroma, heavy juniper, and no alcohol burn to the nasal passages. A sweetish burn to the center of the tongue and some alcohol to the soft palate, with a little heat at the back of the throat. A long finish going from slightly sweet to drier, and a smooth aftertaste.

Corney and Barrows London Distilled Dry Gin, 94.6 proof

Clear and clean, good viscosity, with long legs. A light juniper aroma with strong nasal alcohol attack overlying a light caramel nose. A strong alcohol attack to the tongue with a tangy lemon like sweetness and light juniper/pine flavor. A sweetish aftertaste fades to a medium finish with few other effects.

Crystal Palace Premium London Dry Gin, 80 proof

Clear and clean, decent viscosity, good legs and no color. Very light juniper aroma overlaying a toffee nose with few other scents and a medium alcohol nasal burn. A minty tang comes through the medium alcohol attack to the center of the tongue with a slightly sweet aftertaste that leads to a long finish.

Fleischmann's Extra Dry Gin, 80 proof

Clean and clear with good legs, spirity to the nose with some sinus burn but a clean juniper-coriander nose overall. An initial sweetness in the mouth with some heat along the edges of the tongue and the center of the roof of the mouth. The follow-up reveals a slightly citric feel and a sweetish aftertaste of pine and cedar, some resiny feel, and a long, slightly warm finish.

Gilbey's London Dry Gin, 80 proof

A hint of straw in the color, with standard legs in the glass and some chatoyance. Very light spirity nose with light juniper, and little sinus burn from the alcohol. Juniper in the mouth with a little alcohol on the tip of the tongue and a light lemon zest tartness. A medium finish with a decent aftertaste and fair smoothness with no alcohol burn to the throat.

Glenmore London Dry Gin, 80 proof

Clear and clean, with no discernible color, good viscosity and long legs. A clean nose with a definite hint of lemon zest balanced against the juniper and coriander. In the mouth, the initial sip reveals a definite lemony taste and a smooth tingle on the surface of the tongue, but no heat. The second sip brings out a little heat to the tip and center of the tongue but mostly concentrated around the front of the mouth. The aftertaste still feels lightly of lemon, with a smooth decline to a pleasant mellow finish.

Gordon's London Dry Gin, 80 proof

Good sheeting action, with long clean legs. A strong juniper nose with an astringent feel to the nasal cavity, but no burn. In the mouth there is a slight bitterness evident at the first sip, which slowly ebbs into a smooth feel of juniper, no attack or burn in the mouth, and a good long finish with a pleasantly spirity aftertaste.

Horse Guard London Dry Gin, 80 proof

Clear to the eye, with some legs though a little lighter than most. Very little aroma of either juniper or any other botanical, reminiscent of a vodka but with some unknown aroma joining the alcohol in the nose. A little harsh on the tongue and an attack to the back of the throat. Piney flavor inside the mouth but little aftertaste and a medium duration finish.

Laird's Extra Dry Distilled London Dry Gin, 80 proof

Clean and clear with a light yellow tint, decent viscosity and long legs. Very faint juniper nose with a medium alcohol burn and few other aromas. Smooth sweet taste in the mouth with a light citrus feel and a hint of mint. A sweetish aftertaste which fades to a light burn to the palate and a medium finish.

Leyden's Dry Gin, 80 proof

Very clean in the glass with long legs and light viscosity. A pleasant nose, light in aroma, with just a touch of juniper and no burn to the nose. A light alcohol burn to the inside of the mouth and some attack to the soft palate with burn at the top of the throat. A lingering finish with a pleasantly glowing, smooth aftertaste. Leyden's is even lighter than Bombay Saphire—too light for some tastes—but very fine, and makes a perfect martini.

McCormick Distilled London Dry Gin, 80 proof

Clear and clean with no observable color and long slender legs. The nose reveals a strong gin aroma with juniper, strong lemon zest, and a medium nasal burn. In the mouth the lemon becomes even more evident with a slightly bitter flavor that I can't recognize. It has a slightly chewy and oily mouth feel and some alcohol burn to the tongue. The aftertaste reveals a smooth burn to the throat but few other flavors.

Old Mr. Boston English Market Gin, 80 proof

No color in the glass, with broken legs and light viscosity that sheets down the side of the glass very rapidly. The first nose discovers a light aroma of turpentine or acetone combined with the juniper aroma and very little alcohol burn to the sinuses. The first sip reveals a certain sweetness, with a citric burn to the tip and sides of the front portion of the tongue and no heat as it goes down the throat. The second sip comes forward with a little more alcohol which fills the mouth and stings the palate lightly. The aftertaste has a definite juniper-piney feel in its sweet glow which slowly diminishes over a minute or more, leaving the mouth with a clean taste which invites the next sip.

Plymouth Dry Gin, 82.4 proof

Good legs in a clean glass, light in aroma, with smooth juniper nose. Almost no initial alcohol attack but grows stronger as it rests in and fills up the mouth. Smooth and clean with good mouth feel and no burn down the throat. A good long finish with a pleasant dry aftertaste turning slightly sweet at the end. This excellent gin is wonderfully flavorful and fully deserves its high reputation.

Schlichte Steinhager Dry Gin, 80 proof

Very clear with a little chatoyance and refraction. Very long legs. Dry nose with a hint of herbs almost equaling the juniper and an alcohol burn to the sinus. Very light in the mouth with the alcohol burn starting very slowly and then growing in heat in the center of the tongue. An herbal flavor is almost balanced with the juniper and the finish is long with a neutral aftertaste and tingle which slowly ebbs to a smooth end.

Seagram's Excel Premium Extra Dry Gin, 94 proof

Clean and clear with a light gray-brown tint, good viscosity, and long legs. Light juniper nose with a medium alcohol burn to the nasal passages and few other aromas. Sweet tang of citrus on the first sip with little burn but a light tingle to the center front of the tongue. The second sip shows a little more burn to the entire tongue with a mellow aftertaste leading to a smooth long finish.

Seagram's Extra Dry Gin, 80 proof

Clean and clear, with good legs and viscosity. A hint of lemon or citrus at first nose, with good balance between the juniper and other botanicals Some sinus burn. At first sip there is again a hint of lemon zest, balancing against the juniper and other botanicals with almost no alcohol sting and light attack to the center of the tongue. A little more heat on the second sip, slowly building to a stronger attack with a tingle around the inside of the lips and the center of the tongue. An astringency develops with a slight bitterness toward the back of the throat upon swallowing. The heat remains for some time with a continuing feel of citrus zest which fades slowly to a satisfying finish and a aftertaste that has little effect.

Skol London Dry Gin, 80 proof

To the eye it is clear and clean with slightly broken legs and a not too smooth sheeting action in the glass. The first nosing reveals a whiff of aniseed along with the normal juniper and coriander and little sinus burn. At the second, deeper nosing, the alcohol asserts itself more and the burn to the olfactory nerves seems to abate the licorice-like nose from the first sample. In the mouth the first sip is cool at first with the alcohol being revealed more as the spirit warms. There seems little complexity of either alcohol or botanical, but a slight bitterness is felt as the spirit is swallowed and the aftertaste begins. At the finish, there is a curious neutrality in the aftertaste with a slight feel of licorice and a pleasant feel which slowly ebbs away to a null state.

Tanqueray Dry Gin, 94.6 proof

Clean and clear with long legs and smooth viscosity, sheeting smoothly down the inside of the glass. Good juniper feel to the nose with some alcohol burn to the sinuses. A smooth dry taste in the initial sip, slowly filling the mouth with the burn of alcohol, smoothing out until there is no attack to the throat. The soft palate gets a little heat from the alcohol but it dies away into a long finish and a pleasantly neutral aftertaste which leaves just the memory of juniper.

Tanqueray Malacca Gin, 80 proof

Clean with a slight hint of beige in the coloration, good sheeting action with long legs. The nose reveals a different feel than most gins, with another scent, possibly citrus mingling with but not quite overriding that of the juniper. Some alcohol burn to the sinus is felt but not unpleasantly so. The first sip is almost neutral, and there is little alcohol attack, though the citrus feel carries through lightly. The second sip brings out a little burn but is confined to the center area of the tongue and never reaches the soft palate or the throat. The aftertaste is relatively light and dry with a smooth finish that lingers a surprisingly long time. This is definitely 'something different' among gins; it's among the lighter products and is not as heavily junipered as most, but with a superb flavor.

A Flavored Gin

Seagram's Lime Twisted Gin, 80 proof

All gins are, of course, flavored, but this one has an unusual and conspicuous addition of natural lime flavor. In fact it seems to be just Seagram's gin with added natural lime. To the eye, it is clear and clean with good sheeting action and long legs. To the nose the lime is certainly evident, at first completely blocking the aromas of the other botanicals, but then allowing them through. The lime smell does remain dominant, but slowly the juniper almost regains a balance. The sharpness of the lime is accentuated by the alcohol and the spirit provides a hefty burn for the sinuses. In the mouth, the sweetness of the lime mellows the first sip so that it has an intriguing heat that comes on very slowly and fills the entire mouth, including a light shock to the top of the palate. The aftertaste is also different with the lime predominating and leaving a sweetish burn in the mouth and at the inside of the lips. The juniper is not evident at the finish, but only the lime leaves a fading sweetness with an acrid note as it dies away.

Genevers

Genevers are not yet among my favorite drinks. They take some getting used to, and generally do not mix well. But they do represent a strange and fascinating experience from a bygone age, and should certainly be given a serious trial by any budding connoisseur. The 'jonge' genevers are much more like unflavored vodkas than dry gins, with little discernible juniper.

Bokma Graanjenever Jonge, 70 proof

Clean and clear with a slight hint of beige and long slender legs. A light caramelly nose with little sinus burn. Slightly oily with a little sweetness and a light burn to the outside edges of the tongue. No juniper or other botanicals discernible to either the nose or mouth. The aftertaste reveals a smooth lingering sweetness with little burn and the finish is fairly short.

Bols Corenwyn, 76 proof

Clean with a medium amber gold color and a smooth slide down the inside of the glass. The legs are slender and not long. The nose is reminiscent of a light bourbon with little herbal feel, no detectable juniper, and no burn to the nasal passages. This should perhaps be classified as a schnapps or a vodka rather than a gin. In the mouth there is a definite burn to the lips and the center of the tongue with some sweetness and a little oiliness. The aftertaste is smooth and light with no burn to the throat and is very long and sustained.

Boomsma Jonge, Fine Young Genever Gin, 80 proof

Clear and clean with a hint of gray color and very slender slow legs. The nose shows juniper and a grain base aroma but does not smell like a dry gin, since I can detect none of the other ingredients like lemon zest or coriander. The taste is pleasant and very clean with a strong burn to the tongue and some grain undertones. The aftertaste is pleasant and light with some burn down the throat and a smooth grainy feel, not sweet, but rather clean and lightly sharp.

Boomsma Oude, Fine Old Genever, 80 proof

A pale golden color, yet clear and clean with no visible particulate matter and slender slow moving legs. In the nose the wood is definitely the strongest component with just a hint of the juniper that must be present, and a light nasal burn. In the mouth there is a dryness that seems to be part of the wood flavor and the blending of the flavors seems to be completed for it is all of a whole, with the individual flavors being very difficult to pick out but with a definite feel of aniseed and the underlying grain and wood taste. The aftertaste has little feel or burn and the finish is very short and not very satisfying.

De Kuyper Geneva Gin, 80 proof

This is made from 30 percent grain and 70 percent cane spirits. Clear and clean with broken or no legs. Grainy to the nose with a heavy juniper overtone and a very slight nasal burn. Light in the mouth at first, but rising to a medium burn in the center of the tongue with a toasty burnt undertone and the burn dying away. The aftertaste is surprisingly neutral with almost no burn and a medium long neutral finish.

10

A Little Gin History

Gin was mother's milk to her.

Eliza Doolittle in George Bernard Shaw's *Pygmalion*

Gin is best known today as the main ingredient both of the classic martini and of the gin and tonic—the drink which saved the British Empire by making quinine palatable for the colonial rulers. But gin has a rich and colorful history stretching back through the centuries.

Distillation Comes to Europe

The earliest application of distilling to the manufacturer of beverages was to concentrate the alcohol in wine, using just one distillation. This would have increased the alcoholic strength of the fluid, but only to about 20 percent alcohol by volume (ABV). At first, the key reason for distilling wine was not to make a more strongly alcoholic drink but to reduce the volume of 'wine' that could effectively be transported for long distances (much as fruit juice is today concentrated for cheaper transportation, then diluted again once it's closer to the final consumer). According to legend, the first use of distillation to make alcoholic spirits was accomplished by a Dutch captain, concerned about the amount of space wine was taking up in the hold of his ship. Holland, with its lucrative seaborne trade, became the center of progress in distillation techniques.

The gradual spread of the technology of distillation continued throughout Europe. Wine was distilled into 'eau-de-vie' ('water of life' in French) in Italy and France and barley beer into 'uisge beatha' ('water of life' in Gaelic) in Ireland and Scotland. By the fourteenth century what became known as aquavit, akvavit, or akavit (all modifications of 'water of life' in Latin) was being made in the Baltic and Scandinavian countries. In Russia, Poland, Ukraine, and other countries in the steppes of Eastern Europe, the product of such distillation was called gorzalka or vodka, though before it was called 'vodka', it was called 'zhiznennia voda' which means—you've guessed it—'water of life'.

Secondary distillation processes were introduced by the Dutch, eagerly pursuing the more efficient use of distillation to lower the bulk of their cargoes by taking the water out of wine. The original plan was to reconstitute the wine by putting the water back after the cargo arrived at its destination, but the Dutch found that many consumers liked 'brandeweijn' (burned wine) more without the water than they did if the water were added back. The new product soon became the rage of the Dutch shippers and the consuming public. By the 1500s many different types of spirits were being produced in the Netherlands, including many brandies and liqueurs. The Bols company, still a world-famous spirits producer, was founded in 1575.

Just What the Doctor Ordered

Gin, called 'genever' or 'jenever' (after 'genièvre', French for juniper), was invented around 1650, but juniper was already in use as a food flavoring agent, and had been used to flavor alcoholic drinks. The English king, Henry VI, was drinking some kind of juniper-flavored tipple in the late 1500s. Genever itself was developed and perfected by a man named Franciscus de la Boe (1614–1672). Better known as Dr. Silvius, he was a medical doctor and teaching professor at the University of Leyden. He first manufactured 'jenever' while trying to find a cure for stomach and kidney disorders.

Dr. Silvius knew of the diuretic properties of the juniper berry so he came up with the idea of infusing the oil of the juniper berry into an alcohol base so that it became easier for his patients to consume. He also included other botanical ingredients such as coriander and fennel seed to facilitate some other aspects of digestion and the passage of kidney stones.

While working on his new medicine, he built and kept as many as six small pot stills at his home and in his laboratory to distill the base alcohol which was the prime ingredient for his new medicine. As he tried different formulations and combinations of botanicals, he found that each type of product served to cure different ailments. Some helped with stomach and kidney disorders, others with respiratory problems. Of course, Dr. Silvius did not withhold the benefits of these scientific breakthroughs from his patients.

As word spread through the town and surrounding countryside about this physician and his marvelous new medicine, there was apparently a huge increase in the number of people who reported kidney and stomach disorders. Dr. Silvius found it difficult to keep up with demand for these medicines. Perhaps an agreement was reached between Dr. Sylvius and some of the Dutch distilling companies during this time, to manufacture his new medical discovery, because of the needs of the people and his inability to supply enough product to meet the ever increasing demand. At any rate, commercial production for the non-medical market did get started.

Where the Dutch Got
Their Courage

In the many European wars, the English would sometimes be allied with the Dutch, other times fighting
them. According to some stories, the English were getting their butts whipped whenever they came up against
Dutch troops. The English noticed that before a battle,
the Dutch soldiers could be seen to take sips from small
bottles they kept hanging from their belts. After these little nips the Dutch soldiers went out and fought like crazy
men. The Dutch troops took chances that no sane soldier
would take, but more often than not, they would beat the
English. In other versions of the story, the English and
the Dutch were allies, and the English noticed the same
thing, but from a different aspect. The English began to
call this battle elixir 'Dutch courage'. They got their
hands on some of it, and took it back to England. There
the demand for genever began to grow.

A different story of the introduction of genever to
England concerns the sea battles between the English
and Dutch navies. Beginning in April 1654, the Dutch
were at first defeated in a series of battles with the
English over trading disputes. A treaty was signed
according to which the Dutch were required to render
honors to the British flag before the English would
return the honors. Eventually the naval battles climaxed
in a confrontation between a British squadron and the
Dutch Admiral De Ruyter's fleet off the coast of Oorlam.
The British were finally defeated, ending the odious
treaty and putting the countries back on a level playing
field and at peace. The losing English admiral was given
some genever by the victorious Dutch admiral. This inci-
dent is one more explanation of what may have brought
about the term 'Dutch Courage', and begun the English
fondness for gin.

By 1680, the Dutch were exporting ten million gallons
of genever a year, around the world. In the English
'Glorious Revolution' of 1688, the unpopular English
king James II was deposed, and leading English citizens
invited the Dutch 'stadholder' (king), William of Orange,
to become King of England.

The new king banned the importation of French brandy and raised the customs levies on German wines and spirits, ensuring that most of the distilled spirits sold in England were made by the Dutch. At this time, some English production of genever also began.

The War on Gin

In 1690 the people of London consumed 500,000 gallons of genever. In 1695, taxes on beers and ales made in England were also raised, and the comparatively potent gin became the cheapest alcoholic beverage. During the next 25 years, consumption of genever increased rapidly. The educated classes became aware of lower-class drunkenness, or 'gin madness'. Dram shop advertising included signs proclaiming, 'Drunk for a penny, Dead drunk for two, Clean straw for nothing.'

English law allowed anyone to make and sell gin and it's been claimed that one in every four buildings in the City of London was a gin shop. The public drunkenness of the lower classes began to approach the state of inebriation enjoyed by the gentry, and so the gentry became alarmed.

Water in a city wasn't really fit to drink, and milk was unsanitary before the pasteurization process was developed. Milk being hazardous in its raw state and water being downright dangerous due to infectious diseases, spirits, wine, or beer were the safest drinks. While the rich could afford to drink imported wines, brandies, or ales, the masses could more easily afford gin, so many of them overindulged.

Public drunkenness became perceived as such a problem that Parliament tried to curb drinking through a series of unsuccessful laws beginning in 1729. These laws were ineffective in discouraging gin consumption. By 1750 Londoners were consuming eleven million gallons per year. But in 1751 the 'Tippling Act' was passed, and 'Gin Madness' began to abate.

One of the factors which contributed to the outcry about Gin was a famous woodcut print, *Gin Lane,* by the great artist William Hogarth. This picture depicts a street scene with rampant drunkenness, men passed out in the gutter, women half-dressed and showing their bosoms unclad, and children being allowed to fall into the street below. *Gin Lane* played into the middle-class perception of debauchery and social breakdown among the poor, caused by excessive consumption of gin.

The 'Tippling Act" eliminated the small gin shops and gave the rights of manufacture and distribution of Gin to the larger distillers and retailers. Within ten years, consumption was down to two million gallons a year. Prices rose and quality improved. Gin was no longer so easily available to the poor. With these changes gin was ready to move upscale, into the realm of the rich and powerful. While the consumption of gin by the lower classes was declining, the newer gin companies were consolidating their products and the quality of the spirit was improving.

In England, 'genever' became known as 'gin'. There is a story that in the 1760s, the Dutch firm of De Kuyper sued the British gin manufacturers over their use of the name 'jenever', and won the suit in the English courts. This forced the British manufacturers to stop using the name 'jenever' or 'genever', and they switched over to the name 'gin'. The name may already have been in general use, but the lawsuit may have sealed the permanent change in terminology.

The Brits Like It Strong and Sweet

For the next 60 years gin consumption was mainly controlled by the laws passed by the British Parliament and was fairly stable. Throughout this time gin was still a sweet drink. All gins were normally sweetened with sugar after distillation. One of the most common types of sweet gin was called 'Old Tom'.

Throughout the history of the spirits trade, the British have had a greater influence on the development of different types of spirits than any other people. The original cognac drinkers were mainly the English and the Dutch shippers had the English in mind when they first started distillation of wine. It was also British demand which caused the development and flourishing of the fortified wines (wines with brandy added), Port, Sherry, and Marsala. If you think about the development of all these spirits, you will see that the British like their alcohol strong and sweet.

The next major change in the development of gin happened between 1825 and 1835. Two engineers, Robert Stein of Scotland and Aeneas Coffey of Ireland, invented and patented the continuous-action column still, enabling the distiller to produce much larger quantities of pure alcohol from the same amount of base materials, which could then be converted to gin. This new still meant they could make more alcohol less expensively and improve the quality of the product at the same time.

The original still of this type had a bottom section made of copper which was heated by fire or steam, and the upper portion of the column was made of hardwoods. (I have heard of stills in the Caribbean which still follow this pattern and are used today to make some of the rare rums). This new still allowed the production of a much purer spirit from one distillation run than could be achieved by using many distillations through a pot still. Because of the higher alcohol purity the new still produced, the use of the botanicals began to produce a much drier and more aromatic spirit, with a cleaner aroma and taste.

In the mid-nineteenth century, gin became a respectable drink in British high society, and began being served in gentlemen's clubs. The alcoholic spirit steadily became cleaner and more refined due to the increasing purity of the neutral grain spirits produced by the new distilling process. As the column stills were modified and became still more efficient the aromatic and flavoring elements of the botanicals were allowed to come through even more and the gin became ever more clean and dry.

During this period of change and growth, many of the major gin manufacturers or labels of today started up, grew, or consolidated their businesses. Tanqueray and Gordon's had been in business for some years before they merged in the late 1800s, forming the largest gin company in the world at that time. Other labels such as Beefeater, Booth's, Boodle's, Gilbey's, and many others were founded in the eighteenth and nineteenth centuries and grew much larger in the twentieth.

Around the middle of the nineteenth century, the growth in gin consumption within Great Britain led to the construction of large 'gin palaces' which served many different kinds of gin as well as varying modes of entertainment. During the last quarter of the nineteenth century, the upper crust of society was starting to drink the new 'dry gins', since these had improved in quality. With the introduction of the continuous action still, the bad tasting congeners and fusel oils, which had caused the 'off' flavors, could be removed and a lighter flavored and drier gin produced. This change also allowed the tastes of the botanicals to come through more readily and increased the complexity and quality of the gin.

The expansion of the British Empire also contributed to the growth of gin consumption. In the 1870s, at far-flung outposts in the tropics, gin became the staple to mix with and somewhat alleviate the taste of the quinine in tonic water. Quinine was the main medicine used to combat the malaria which was everywhere in tropical climes. By this time, the origin of gin itself as a medical treatment had largely been forgotten, but it was embraced as a way to help the anti-malarial medicine, quinine, go down.

The Birth of the Martini

There are many conflicting legends about the advent of that most mystical of gin cocktails, the martini. In the 1860s, Jerry Thomas, a bartender at the Occidental Hotel in San Francisco, mixed up a new cocktail he dubbed the 'Martinez', for a customer who was going to that town, located on the other side of San Francisco bay. The new drink consisted of bitters, maraschino, vermouth, ice, and 'Old Tom' (sweet gin). In 1912, Martini di Arma di Taggia, a bartender at New York's Hotel Knickerbocker, invented a drink using equal parts of gin and dry vermouth, a dash of bitters, and a twist of lemon peel. This is the version which is generally accepted as having evolved into the martini that millions have been drinking for the last 80 years.

On August 16, 1920, the Volstead Act went into effect, closing down the legal manufacture and distribution of all alcoholic beverages and bringing in the 'speakeasy' and the 'bootleg booze' era. While prohibition effectively limited the wine, whiskey, beer, and brandy trades, gin flourished under the new restrictions.

Gin was the easiest spirit to produce illegally, needing only industrial potable alcohol and the botanical flavoring additives plus a place to mix it. The bathtub in an apartment would do just fine, being able to hold 20 gallons of alcohol with ease, so gin became the king of illegal liquors under Prohibition. It did so mainly because of its ease of manufacture, ready availability, and the ease with which it could be drunk straight, or mixed as a martini or some other cocktail. Sales of martinis increased and other mixed drinks using gin boomed during the years of prohibition.

Vodka would have been even easier to make, but the gin botanicals may have been useful in concealing some unpleasant congeners in the alcohol that was available, and there was no tradition of vodka-drinking in America at that time.

In 1934, the Volstead Act was repealed and the manufacture and sale of alcoholic drinks again became legal without a doctor's prescription. President Franklin Delano Roosevelt welcomed the end of prohibition by drinking a martini made to his own recipe (two parts gin to one part vermouth, with a teaspoon of olive brine, served with an olive, and the rim of the glass rubbed with lemon peel). For the next few years, drinking was made much of in the popular media of the time, with movies and radio showing and telling how the upper crust lived.

Since this was the depression era, few people could afford to live that way but the depictions may have cheered up those who watched.

One of the most popular series of movies from the 1930s was the 'Thin Man' mysteries, starring William Powell and Myrna Loy, in which the drinking was continuous and the performances of the cast members (even the dog Asta) amusing and a little campy. The antics of the stars in these mystery-comedies were a source of endless entertainment, and may have contributed to the feeling of the era that drinking alcohol was legitimate and amusing.

During World War II, consumption of all alcoholic drinks either ceased or declined somewhat, for the alcohols consumed were those that had been made before the war. Prices remained much the same even though the manufacture of alcoholic beverages was down because of the war effort. After the war was over, the men who came home were eager to relax, forget the horrors of the past, and revel in the brightness of the future, until they were interrupted again by the fighting in Korea. After that 'police action' was completed, the country tried to resettle into life and take up where it had left off. In the 1950s the cocktail hour became a standard feature of American life, and the three-martini lunch became a staple of American business.

The 1960s we all know as the time of the hippie, race riots, and college youths spreading 'flower power', 'free love', and protests against the war in Viet Nam. Songs and slogans promoted the use of marijuana and other illegal drugs, which tended to discourage the idea of drinking alcohol. Those who use marijuana or other illegal drugs are usually not especially drawn to alcoholic beverages.

The 1970s were the time of the 'Status Quo' and few changes happened outside of the political wars within the U.S., and the resignation of President Nixon following Watergate. The entertainment industry and the consumption of alcoholic beverages continued apace and the Cold War rolled along, but there were few shooting wars, even though the Iran Hostage crisis tortured the country. The growth of vodka consumption and the development of the vodka martini were cutting into the sales of gin.

In the 1980s Americans became more health-conscious and began to cut down on their consumption of alcohol, and vodka overtook gin as the most-consumed form of spirits. During the 1990s, the overall market for spirits has declined (by over 15 percent from 1986 to 1997), and consumers are prepared to pay more for better-quality spirits.

Where Gins Are Going

Today, consumers are more concerned to know what they are putting inside their bodies. People are eating better food than ever and they now seem to be trying to drink better-quality alcoholic beverages. They are trying to learn about the spirits that are available throughout the world and that process can be difficult and very expensive. Undoubtedly the gins available to Americans today are among the best ever made.

The newest of the new gins seem to feature the great acceptance of the lighter version of Bombay Dry, Sapphire, with the new Dutch gin "Leyden" trying to gain a portion of that same market. And yet there are those who still prefer the heavier gins, hence the re-introduction of Plymouth in 1998. The 1998 introduction of Citadelle gin may even begin a new run of more botanicals being used in gins, since it uses 19 different herbs and spices, the most of any gin in the marketplace of which I am aware. This gin is very flowery, with strong floral accents in the aroma, taste and aftertaste. Perhaps this new style gin will start a countertrend to the 'dry' direction of recent years.

While sales of American-made gins are falling, many imported gins are increasing their sales. When you take into account the new gins that are now being introduced, gins like Leyden, Citadelle, Tanqueray Malacca, and Bombay Sapphire, you have to conclude that gin is going to be around for many years, helped by the rebirth of the martini.

Where gin may go in the future is difficult to predict. The liquor market is highly competitive and constantly changing, with new products appearing almost every day, many of them ultimately disappearing, but others winning the affections of the consumers. I believe that gin is one of the most reliable and enduring categories of spirits, because of its clean, bright aroma, smooth, crisp taste, and the perennial interest in gin cocktails.

PART III

The Art of Living with Gins and Vodkas

11

How to Organize a Gin or Vodka Tasting

The number of those who undergo the fatigue of judging for themselves is very small indeed.

Richard Brinsley Sheridan, *The Critic*

It's easy enough to have a few friends round, open a few bottles of gin or vodka, and casually swap impressions about what you're drinking. Not that there's anything wrong with that, but holding a serious tasting takes somewhat more knowledge and commitment, and will yield far more satisfaction. Like a posse, a tasting is something you have to *organize*.

For the initial things you should do to set up a tasting, I suggest that you check out the largest liquor store close to your home. Go in and see what they have, both in the way of glassware and the different labels within the types of liquors you wish to explore. You might also check as to any condiments or unusual food items you may wish to serve your fellow tasters. Many liquor stores also sell specialty food items which might suit your needs. As to your guests, a group of six to ten would be optimal, but ten to twenty would not be unusual. Especially if you invite couples.

Try to avoid the Russian habit of putting vodka in the freezer. This practice makes it very difficult to get the true tastes and aromas out of the spirit. Frozen vodka means frozen taste buds, so keep it at room temperature.

The Objective of the Tasting

Each tasting you organize should have a clear goal. Naturally, your first tasting might merely be to compare five or six leading vodkas or gins. As you become more experienced, you will want to specialize, for example, comparing three Polish with three Russian vodkas, or three light gins with three more traditional gins. Your tasting should have a theme. The idea is that at the end of the tasting, you will all have learned something you didn't know at the start.

I have seen wine tastings that included over a hundred different labels, but these were samplings of products that suppliers wanted to sell to a grocery company and were for the purpose of picking out the outstanding products from among those being considered. The type of tasting that you might hold at your home, or in a room in a local restaurant, will be far more intimate and far more focussed.

You and your guests should each taste all of the drinks, one after the other, at the same time. You should all make notes as you taste, then later compare notes and discuss your conclusions. The number of drinks should be between four and eight. Six is usually optimal. Unless you are going to take the heroic course of never swallowing, your judgment will begin to suffer slightly after even a few small sips of vodka or gin.

At the beginning of the tasting, you should briefly explain aloud to the assembled guests what the purpose or theme is. It helps if you can dramatize this in some way, for example by displaying maps of the regions from which the drinks have originated.

It almost goes without saying that if you organize any function the purpose of which is to consume alcohol, you have some moral responsibility to ensure that your guests have safe travel arrangements to get home at the end.

Glassware for a Tasting

The glassware you use is vitally important, especially with gins and vodkas, where the differences among labels may often be extremely subtle and elusive.

I once organized a tasting in a Mexican restaurant for a group of people who wanted to learn about fine tequilas. The restaurant provided everyone with plenty of four-ounce old-fashioned glasses, but I took along my own five-ounce piece of stemware called a chimney glass. Whenever a tequila was poured, I put some in my glass and went round the room, asking everyone to smell the contents of their own glass and then of mine. The difference was often so great that some of the people there couldn't believe, at first, that they were really smelling the same spirit.

A proper tasting glass should be about five to six ounces in capacity, and rather tall and slender in shape. This allows your nose to detect the aromas without getting too much alcohol burn in your sinus cavities. It also allows the shape of the glass to trap the majority of the aromas in the glass itself. Short, squat glasses are not so effective for nosing or tasting spirits, because the aromas dissipate from the wide mouth. So avoid 'shot' glasses whenever you can.

My recommendation is the 'chimney' glass, if you can find it. It's a stemmed glass about five inches high. The container portion is three inches and the stem two inches. The widest portion of the bowl, at the bottom, is two inches wide, and the chimney is one inch wide. The bottom of the bowl curves to the widest point, and then curves back to narrow slightly, and rises on a narrowing curve for an inch, then straight up for another inch. I've also heard this kind of glass referred to as a 'miniature hurricane glass'.

If you can't get a chimney glass, a cognac glass will also serve, as will a six-ounce wine glass similar to a champagne flute. Any glass which will concentrate the aromas and still keep your nose away from the surface of the spirit will suffice, but a brandy snifter is not my favorite since it has the tendency to concentrate the aromas without maintaining the necessary distance from the surface of the spirit. The spirit can seem a little 'hot' when nosing in a brandy snifter. A good glass may be hard to find. Libbey Glass Co. used to make the chimney glass as a matter of course, but they have stopped making it and you can only occasionally find it in a restaurant supply house. Some whiskeys do supply the glass in question with some of their spirits (notably the Glenmorangie sampler pack), but these glasses are made in Europe or Mexico.

Cleanliness is also very important, since a glass which retains any traces of other drinks will contaminate the tasting and prevent the taster from identifying the true character of the drink. Even if the glass has been unused for some time, it is important that all glasses being used be washed and rinsed in non-chlorinated water before the tasting event. Obviously, each glass has to be completely cleaned and rinsed between each different drink at the tasting, or you must begin with a supply of several clean glasses per person. Never, of course, use plastic 'glasses': aside from their inelegance, the petroleum that most polyurethane hard-plastic glasses are made from will interfere with the aromas and subtle tastes of the spirits.

Water and Nibbles

There should always be bottled spring water or distilled water available, since the chlorine in tap water deadens the nose and taste buds, and the bubbles in seltzer or soda water can disguise the actual flavor of the spirit.

Bottled water should always be available for the tasters, not just for the cleansing of the palate after tasting one of the spirits in question, but to mix with the spirit in the glass and bring out both the good and the bad aromas and tastes inherent in the product under consideration. Many of the by-products of distillation are not soluble in water and will be forced to make their presence known by the addition of water to bring down the proof strength of the spirit. An amount of water equal to the amount of spirit in the glass should be sufficient for this purpose.

Some type of easy-to-handle food should be available between drinks, to provide a contrast and help erase the palate of the memory of the earlier drinks. For Russian or any vodkas, caviar of one sort or another can never be amiss. Some of the U.S. domestic caviars are not too expensive. Otherwise try dips and chips or other hors d'oeuvres, so that you allow each member of the party to take their time and savor the intricacies of the different tastes and aromas. But always remember that some structure must be maintained at such an affair and this can be difficult when sampling spirits.

Gins and vodkas both go very well with just about any salty food that doesn't have too many competing flavors. Vodkas go with anything that can be considered remotely Russian or Polish in origin, from borscht to caviar, lox and bagels to motza ball soup, all will show a different side when consumed with vodka, or even with gin.

The Choice of Liquors

You must first decide whether your tasting will be of gins or of vodkas. If you decide to try the gins, there are the domestics and the imports, with the majority of the imports coming from England. The domestics are somewhat different, though many brand labels started life as imports and the recipe for that particular product has simply moved to this country under license. Gilbey's, Gordon's, and Booth's all migrated to the U.S. in this manner, after starting in Britain.

One idea for a gin tasting is to try the domestic transplants against the gins still made in England. For example, the three listed above, and any three of either Bombay Dry, Tanqueray, Plymouth, Boodle's, Beefeater's, or any other imported gins would be a good starting point.

I wouldn't try the 'Tanqueray Malacca' gin at first, since its primary flavor is decidedly different from those traditional gins which use juniper as their main botanical flavoring agent. The same holds true for both Leyden and Bombay Sapphire, but mainly because they are more lightly junipered gins, and should be compared against each other rather than against the fuller flavored or more heavily junipered gins.

However, these three would be very interesting to compare against one another as a trial and even against some of the others, after your group has had a chance to try tasting some of the less differentiated gins. You and your guests should make an effort to learn what the normal taste of gin is supposed to be, before you start trying the non-traditional new breed of gins. And that is where the three listed above would fall: Bombay Sapphire, Leyden, and Tanqueray Malacca are all decidedly non-traditional

For vodkas, it seems that the four sub-groups into which I have divided them (Russian, Polish, American, and Western European) would make a good starting point. Most of the Russian labels, it must be remembered, can be made by any of the ten distilleries in Russia, and as a result the quality of these products may vary within the label itself. Since Stolichnaya can be made in any of those plants, to some extent you take your chances. Always remember that, with almost any drink, actual differences in quality between different bottles of the same label *may* account for different opinions among different tasters.

Poland has a similar problem, though not as severe as Russia. Since three of the major brands, Luksusowa, Wyborowa, and Extra Zytnia, are controlled by Agros, this group makes sure that the quality of those brands is maintained. The super-premium label, Chopin, is made only at the polmos in Siedlce, under very strict quality controls. The same holds true for other Polish labels, like Krolewska, Original Polish, and Belvedere.

Another tasting 'theme' would be to compare the different base ingredients among the vodkas. For example, try two potato vodkas versus two rye vodkas and an additional two wheat or grain mixture vodkas. This would allow you to judge the different ingredients against each other, as well as against products using the same basic raw materials.

Alternatively, your tasting could compare Russian, Polish, Western European, and U.S. vodkas against each other. Say, two from each country. Possibilities from the U.S. would be Skyy and Smirnoff; from Poland, Wyborowa and Krolewska; from Russia, Stolichnaya and Priviet; and from Europe, Finlandia and Tanqueray Sterling. Just remember that the differences between these products can be very subtle and that you should take your time.

Another approach would be to move up to the imports in either of the two categories. For the gins; Tanqueray, Plymouth, Beefeater's, Cork Dry, Bombay, and Old Raj might be a good grouping (Old Raj might be a little expensive, being priced at over $50), with Bombay Sapphire, Leyden, and Tanqueray Malacca being another good grouping.

The vodkas give you a little more leeway than the gins, simply because they have more types and labels to choose from, with Ketel One, Blavod's Black Vodka, Finlandia, Absolut, French Alps, Grey Goose, Mezzaluna, and other outstanding vodkas in the European group alone.

The four basic groups of vodkas should supply enough different combinations to keep your tastings going for quite some time, especially if you cross check between the styles and categories. With over 100 different labels of vodkas available (including the flavoreds) and over 40 gins, at six to eight labels per tasting, it could take quite some time for you and your friends to determine what gin or vodka you thought was best.

How to Taste

There is a right way to taste, and if any of your guests are beginners, you should explain this procedure at the outset, reminding them if necessary as the tasting proceeds.

First, you hold the glass up to the light and examine the appearance of the spirit for clarity, color, or any unusual characteristics. You also observe the 'legs', the appearance the spirit makes as it washes against the inside of the glass.

Second is the aroma or 'nose'. The sense of smell makes an important contribution to the sense of taste—that's why, if you have a bad cold, you can't taste anything properly: onion soup tastes like nothing more than hot, salty water. But the aroma also has independent importance, before the spirit hits your tastebuds.

Third, you sip the drink gently and closely examine the taste and any other sensations, like the characteristic 'burn' of alcohol. This will change over time, as the spirit spreads through your mouth. Concentrate attentively as the flavor and aroma move through your mouth and nostrils. Don't take a sip and then start chattering; this is serious business. Swallow the spirit, still closely observing the total effect.

Does the flavor and sensation fill the whole mouth or seem to affect only parts of it? How sweet or dry is it? Is the flavor complex? It will take practice before you can distinguish qualities intrinsic to the spirit from accidents of the way it happens to hit your mouth. Also with practice, you will gradually learn to notice certain recurring taste components, and to identify them, mentally separating them from any other components you cannot, as yet, give a name to.

Finally, there is the finish or aftertaste. This can differ surprisingly from the initial taste, and can be long or short. A long finish, lasting several seconds, is to be preferred.

At each stage—appearance, nose, initial taste, and finish—the individual tasters should write down their observations. *Drinks, like dreams, must be written down immediately if they are to be analyzed, or they are quickly lost.* Making the effort to record the experiences in words actually trains one's senses to discriminate more subtly, and should therefore be pursued religiously, even if at first it seems pointless or comical. A written record is also important because human beings are amazingly susceptible to becoming confused about their experiences, so they will often mix up their recent recollections of smells and tastes. By the fifth drink, the taster may not be too sure about whether it was the first or the second that had that peculiar spicy quality.

So every taster starts with a pad and pencil, and must be expected to make notes on each drink. The notes can be merely scribbled jottings, as long as the writer can refer to them and decipher them.

To help your guests record their impressions, you could design and print up a 'tasting form' on your computer. The collected forms could then be saved and used for comparisons in subsequent tastings.

After writing down their impressions, the assembled tasters usually want to discuss them and compare impressions. They must be discouraged from saying merely that they like or dislike a particular spirit. What is it that they like or dislike about it? Is the nose complex or crude? Is the taste smooth or rough, dry or sweet? Is the finish satisfyingly long or disappointingly short?

As well as comparing their own impressions, they can also open a book like this one, or tasting notes from a beverage magazine, and compare their own impressions with those of the absent writer. Of course, the aim is not necessarily to arrive at a unanimous decision as to who is right, but it's surprising how often unanimity or near-unanimity is easily reached.

Individual palates develop over time. These drinks are very subtle and sensing the differences between them can be difficult, particularly the vodkas. Most people will probably not be able to tell the difference between some of the vodkas at the first sampling. After the first trial, subsequent nosings and tastings should produce quick improvement in identifying the factors that make the products different.

The gins shouldn't cause any problem, since the botanicals will be the main focus of aroma and taste, and every gin's own botanicals are unique, but being able to tell two vodkas of the same category apart may take some time.

How to Conduct the Tasting

As to the amount of spirit that should be tasted, use very small quantities, just enough to swirl in the glass to release the aroma of the spirit in question. Probably the optimum amount would be a quarter ounce or less. A quarter ounce of spirit is plenty to allow your guests to nose and taste it.

As an alternative to sipping the spirit direct, a cocktail straw might be used to sample very small amounts. This can be accomplished by inserting the straw in the spirit, placing your finger over the other end of the straw using the vacuum to hold the spirit in the straw, and then placing the straw in your mouth and removing your finger. You will be able to control the amount of alcohol you consume much more precisely using this method.

The most dedicated tasting purists will not swallow any liquor; they will use a spittoon. But except on special occasions for connoisseurs, you will do that only alone and in private.

If you present the groups of spirits for tasting in a logical order, you will find that it is also easier to remember the decisions made as to each label. Blind tastings can be very useful in separating actual experience from expectations. Only you will know the names of the labels; your guests will have to make comments without any clues from what they may have heard about the label they are commenting on. But most often an 'open' selection is best, especially as most of these labels are not going to be already familiar to your guests. You could also vary slightly by having a basically open tasting with one 'mystery' item.

In an open tasting, you line up your bottles along a table, with a card in front of each bottle indicating the order in which they are to be tasted. Let everyone who is involved in the tasting get their tasting sample of each selection before the testing by eye, nose and mouth begins. After the first run-through of all types, you may return to those you have particularly liked or disliked, to reassess your position. As you nose, taste, and evaluate each label, write down your impressions of each product and later go back to check your first impressions.

After you have gone through the first flight, stop and let everyone talk out what they thought of each label. Make a sort of game out of the evaluation, by letting everyone express themselves about the products and by tallying a total of the impressions of everyone present. Make sure you keep records of the overall choices of the evaluators, and either collect them at the end of each session, or ask them to hang onto their tasting cards until the end of the entire process. You will find that, over several tastings, many impressions will change. The favorites of the first day may move down the chart and some of those not well thought of will improve, as the palates of the tasters become more discriminating over time.

And that is after all, the only way to find out which spirits are best for you, taste and evaluate them yourself. Don't take anyone else's word for what spirit is best, not even mine. And remember that price is not a reliable indicator. Some very reasonably priced products are at least as good and sometimes better than products priced much higher. Taste them yourself. You can use this book and other printed sources as indicators of directions which you might try, but my tastes may not be the same as yours. There are as many different opinions about all types of products as there are products and people who use or consume them.

12
A Cosmos of Cocktails

The knives and forks jingled on the tables as we sped through the darkness; the little circle of gin and vermouth in the glasses lengthened to oval, contracted again, with the sway of the carriage, touched the lip, lapped back again, never spilt; I was leaving the day behind me. Julia pulled off her hat and tossed it into the rack above her, and shook her night-dark hair with a little sigh of ease—a sigh fit for the pillow, the sinking firelight and a bedroom window open to the stars and the whisper of bare trees.

Evelyn Waugh, *Brideshead Revisited*

Gin appeared in the mid-seventeenth century, but the history of the cocktail began over 200 years later. People had been drinking mixtures of alcoholic beverages and various other substances such as fruit juices for thousands of years, but the actual process of having a cocktail mixed up in a tavern by a bartender began after the middle of the nineteenth century.

Gin entered the world as genever, and evolved into the sweetened product sometimes called 'Old Tom'. But the cocktail era started only after gin had further developed into something very like today's dry gins. While the growing acceptance of the drier gins allowed the full flavors and aromas of the botanicals to come through, it also allowed the flavors and aromas of the various mixers to meld with the gin in such a way that they became parts of a harmonius unity. The mixer was no longer overpowered by the base flavor of the gin or genever, but rather merged in such a way that the spirit and the mixer were both enhanced by the presence of the other portion of the drink.

While many different styles of drinks were developed utilizing gin, other types of spirits were also tried in cocktails. Bourbon and brandy were certainly used in such drinks as the Manhattan and the Alexander, but those were developments of the 1900s; the mixed drinks of the late 1800s were almost always made with gin.

One of the earliest mixed drinks was the gin and tonic. Many have regarded it as 'the perfect cocktail'. Most sources would agree that this drink began in the tropical lands then colonized by the British Empire, as a more palatable way to take your quinine. The strangely evocative appeal of this drink with such a utilitarian origin may be caused by the contrasting or even competing flavors of the components, just as a little salt can sometimes make sweet things, like watermelon, seem even sweeter. By a stroke of luck, the combination of sugar and quinine with the smooth complexity of the gin brings all of the elements of this noble cocktail into one majestic composition.

In the tropical areas of Egypt, India, Malaya, Borneo, Africa, Australia and other torrid provinces of the British Empire, having your five o'clock gin and tonic signalled the end of the work day and was the perfect way to relax before dinner. After you had consumed your medicine and your dinner, the men would usually switch over to some other type of drink, probably cognac or scotch, as the dinner settled and the evening cooled, and the women might enjoy a pink gin. The beginnings of 'the cocktail hour' can be discerned in the British introduction of the gin and tonic in the nineteenth century.

The Martini Legend

In the early twentieth century, cocktails rapidly became more widespread, with the most popular of the gin cocktails emerging as the 'martini' during the period from the 1910s to the 1930s. As with most cocktails, there are innumerable different stories about how, where, and when the martini was invented. Perhaps the earliest reference to a cocktail with a similar name is in a bartender's guide from 1887, which gives the recipe for a cocktail called the 'Martinez', a drink composed of gin, orange bitters, sweet vermouth, and either triple sec or maraschino. This drink may have been first invented and served by bartender Jerry Thomas (the author of the 1887 book) in San Francisco, to a customer who was taking the ferry to the small town of Martinez on the other side of San Francisco bay.

There's another story about a gold miner who in 1874 bought some whiskey in a bar in the town of Martinez. He wanted a little something extra for the sack of gold nuggets he used to pay for the bottle. So the bartender (Julio Richelieu) fixed him a small cocktail. When he asked what it was, the bartender told him it was a 'Martinez'. There is a commemorative plaque on the corner of two main streets in Martinez, announcing that Martinez is the birthplace of the martini.

There was another cocktail with the right ingredients for a martini but the wrong name. A drink called the 'Marquerite' cocktail, whose recipe appeared in print in 1896, was composed of "1 dash of orange bitters, 2/3 Plymouth Gin, 1/3 French vermouth". This is probably the earliest reference to a drink similar to the modern martini, though the name is different.

Probably the most accepted version of the martini's origin is the one attributed to Signor Martini di Arma di Taggia, who was head bartender at the Knickerbocker Hotel in New York City during the early 1910s. It's often claimed that he is the inventor of the 'dry martini', using half-and-half imported dry gin and French Noilly Prat vermouth, with a drop of orange bitters.

Today of course, such would be considered a very 'wet' martini; the accepted formula for a dry martini now is from four to eight parts dry gin to one part vermouth. Then there are the homeopathic recipes, that call for such things as waving the vermouth cork over the gin in the martini glass, looking at a bottle of dry vermouth while pouring the gin into the shaker or stirring glass or passing the bottle of dry gin around the bottle of vermouth while both are still sealed. The only question raised by such recipes is why so many people find it embarrassing to admit that they like to drink straight gin.

A more credible approach to the correct proportions of the two primary ingredients to make the driest martini, is the one which calls for a pitcher to be filled with ice, two measures of dry vermouth poured in, stirred, and the vermouth poured off. The gin is then added to pick up the flavor of the vermouth from the ice left in the pitcher. The final trick to the serving, calls for the martini to be strained into a martini glass, an olive or an onion added, and the drink handed to the consumer. In the beginning, a martini always had a dash of Angostura or orange bitters added, but now such an addition is almost extinct.

Don't Forget the Vermouth

Everyone's always concerned about the gin used to make the martini, but few people ever give much thought to the vermouth, which is the second most important part of a martini. What is vermouth, you say? 'I never use it anyway when I make a dry martini.' Well then, you're not drinking a martini; you're drinking your gin straight. A martini must include some amount of dry or white vermouth, no matter how minuscule, or it isn't a martini.

Vermouth is a wine, made from grapes and fortified with a grape-based distillate (brandy), to bring it to a normal alcoholic strength between 16 and 21 percent alcohol. It's normally considered an aperitif if drunk by itself, which it often is in Europe. It serves to clean the consumer's mind and spirit of the dusty travails of the day, and prepare for the coming evening. Vermouth is aromatized, which means that, like gin, it has botanicals added to it, many of which are also used to flavor gin. Many more botanicals may be used to flavor vermouth than to flavor gin, but juniper is not usually one of vermouth's ingredients.

So mixing vermouth with gin is somewhat like intensifying the botanicals with the additional herbs and spices contained in the vermouth. That's why some serious drinkers think it best not to overdo the vermouth, for too many additional aromas and tastes may distract from those that the gin maker has included. But if you want your martini to be even more complex, feel free to add as much vermouth as it takes.

A martini should be called a martini only when it is made with gin. And a dry martini must contain both dry gin and some discernible amount of dry vermouth, no matter how tiny. If you wish to ration your vermouth with an eyedropper, it can still be called a martini, but if there is no vermouth included in the drink, then it is straight gin. Or in the case of a vodka marty, straight vodka. But a true martini can be made only with gin.

In my opinion the gin producers should take a leaf out of the book of the tequila distillers, who waged a successful legal battle to prevent the selling of a mixed drink called a 'margarita', when it contained no tequila. The changing of the original drink, the martini, into some other concoction that has no reference to what the name is associated with is tantamount to blasphemy. That's why drinks are named, so that the person doing the ordering understands what type of drink they're going to get. If the name 'martini' is used for drinks other than the original mixture, then a name means nothing. Trademarks are worthless and a person can call himself anything he or she likes with no repercussions. The martini should be, as it has been since its first incarnation, the epitome of elegance and class, the driest, cleanest, and smoothest drink ever poured into a glass.

The Magic of the Martini

For the martini drinker, the afternoon slowly slides into evening and the evening into night, with nothing to threaten the ambiance of the moment. If you're alone while drinking martinis, perhaps the drink is to make you forget. If with a group of two or more, it will surely provoke conversation and thought, at least until the third, after which the discussion becomes less consequential.

A martini can drown the misfortunes of unrequited love or sanctify the beginning of a new relationship, hide sorrow or amplify joy, conjure up a despondency for discussion among friends, or put a lampshade on your head in an effort to make everyone else have as much fun as you're having. Whatever the time of day or the mood of the person drinking this most classic of drinks, the martini will enhance it.

From the beginning, at whatever place the first approximation of the martini was consumed, it has grown in fame and shrunk in the challenge of newcomers to the cocktail wars, but it has always held on to a certain group of those who love its stylish audacity and cherish its austere mystique.

The martini grew in power and fame during that shameful episode called Prohibition, when good law-abiding citizens became law-breakers because of misguided attempts to legislate morality by the religiously conservative congress. On the occasion of the repeal of the detestable Volstead Act in 1934, the president, Franklin Delano Roosevelt, consumed a martini of his own recipe to celebrate the ending of this wretched period of repression. His standard recipe was two parts gin to one part vermouth, with a teaspoon of olive brine, but he did experiment occasionally, sometimes adding anisette for a licorice touch or even a few drops of fruit juice to sweeten the drink.

Throughout the rest of the 1930s and on into the seventies, the martini remained the drink of choice for many businessmen, and was only replaced as the unquestioned champion of the cocktail age by the unexpected and irresistible rise of the margarita in the late 1970s. But the martini is too tough to slink off quietly into history. The resurrection of the martini has begun.

The younger set are once again fascinated by this most elegant of cocktails, and they are continually attempting to make it their own. Unfortunately, they are often really trying out new styles of drinks and calling them 'martinis', when these new drinks should be given new names of their own. There are now something of the order of 100 cocktails that make use of the name 'martini' without employing *any* of the base ingredients used in the preparation of a real martini.

One such creation is also called the 'marstini', and comprises different species of chocolate, including Crème de Cacao, chocolate syrup, and bits of frozen Mars candy bars. Sounds more like a soda fountain confection than a martini to me, but some people will drink anything. Apparently the current determination of what makes something a martini is only whether it can be poured into a standard martini glass.

Now to conclude our exploration of vodkas and gins, let's take a look at some of the classic cocktail recipes that have withstood the ravages of the years, plus a few of the newer imbibables that have been dreamed up more recently.

Gin Cocktails

Martinez
$1\frac{1}{2}$ ounce gin
$1\frac{1}{2}$ ounce sweet vermouth
1 dash orange bitters
1 T maraschino syrup
Pour over ice in tall glass, stir.

Martini
$1\frac{1}{2}$ ounce dry gin
$\frac{3}{4}$ ounce dry vermouth
Mix in cocktail shaker or pitcher, strain into martini glass, garnish if wished.

Gin and Tonic
2 ounces gin
Good quality tonic water
Ice
Fill a tall, straight-sided glass with ice, add gin, fill
   with tonic.

Tom Collins
2 ounces gin
Juice of $\frac{1}{2}$ lemon
1 t powdered sugar
Club soda
Shake with ice, strain into glass, add club soda, stir.

Gin Buck
$1\frac{1}{2}$ ounce gin
Juice of $\frac{1}{2}$ lemon
Ginger ale
Pour gin and lemon juice into glass over ice, fill with
   ginger ale, stir.

Gin Rickey
$1\frac{1}{2}$ ounce Gin
Juice of $\frac{1}{2}$ lime
Club soda
Pour gin and lime juice into glass over ice, fill with
   club soda, stir.

Singapore Sling
$1\frac{1}{2}$ ounces gin
$\frac{1}{2}$ ounce cherry brandy or Cherry Herring
$\frac{1}{2}$ ounce Benedictine
1 t sugar syrup (half sugar, half water)
Club soda
Juice of $\frac{1}{2}$ lemon
Shake lemon, sugar, and gin with ice, strain into tall
   glass over ice, fill with club soda, float cherry
   brandy on top serve with straws and garnish.

Grand Royal Fizz
2 ounces gin
Juice of $\frac{1}{2}$ lemon
Juice of $\frac{1}{2}$ orange
1 t powdered sugar
2 t light cream
$\frac{1}{2}$ t maraschino syrup
Club soda
*Shake with ice and strain into glass, fill with club
   soda, stir.*

Gin Sour
2 ounces gin
Juice of $\frac{1}{2}$ lemon
$\frac{1}{2}$ t powdered sugar
*Shake with ice, strain into sour glass, garnish with
   slice of lemon, cherry.*

Gin & Bubbles
2 ounces gin
Juice of $\frac{1}{2}$ lemon
2 t powdered sugar
Chilled champagne
*Stir in Collins glass, add ice, and fill with champagne,
   stir, and garnish.*

Golden Fizz
2 ounces gin
1 ounce lemon or lime juice
1 t sugar syrup
1 egg yolk
Club soda
Lemon or lime slice
*Mix ingredients over ice in shaker or blender, pour
   into glass and fill with soda, garnish.*

Ramos Fizz
2 ounces gin
$\frac{3}{4}$ ounce lemon juice
$\frac{3}{4}$ t sugar syrup
$\frac{1}{2}$ ounce heavy cream or half-and-half
Several dashes orange flower water
1 egg white
Club soda
Mix ice and ingredients in blender, fill with soda, and
  stir.

Bee's Knees
1 $\frac{1}{2}$ ounces gin
1 t honey
Lemon juice to taste
Mix with ice in shaker or blender, strain into glass.

Bronx Cocktail
1 $\frac{1}{2}$ ounces gin
$\frac{1}{2}$ ounce orange juice
Dash dry vermouth
Dash sweet vermouth
Shake with ice, strain into glass.

Gin Sidecar
1 $\frac{1}{2}$ ounces gin
$\frac{3}{4}$ ounce Triple Sec
1 ounce lemon juice
Shake or blend with ice, pour into cold
  old-fashioned glass.

Gin Sling
2 ounces gin
1 ounce lemon juice
1 ounce sugar or orgeat syrup
Club soda or water
Mix in double old-fashioned glass, fill with club soda
  or water.

Hawaiian Orange Blossom
$1\frac{1}{2}$ ounces gin
1 ounce Curaçao
2 ounces orange juice
1 ounce pineapple juice
Shake with ice and strain into sour glass.

Green Dragon
$1\frac{1}{2}$ ounces gin
1 ounce green crème de menthe
$\frac{1}{2}$ ounce kümmel
$\frac{1}{2}$ ounce lemon juice
Several dashes bitters
Shake or blend, strain into glass.

Lumberjack
1 ounce gin
$\frac{1}{2}$ ounce applejack
$\frac{1}{2}$ ounce Southern Comfort
$\frac{1}{2}$ ounce maple syrup
Shake with ice, strain into chilled cocktail glass.

Orange Blossom
$1\frac{1}{2}$ ounce gin
1 ounce orange juice
Slice orange
*Shake with ice, strain into cold glass, garnish with
  orange slice.*

Vodka Cocktails

Black Russian
2 ounces vodka
1 ounce Kahlúa
Pour over ice in old-fashioned glass.

White Russian
2 ounces vodka
1 ounce Kahlúa
Cream or half-and-half
Pour vodka and Kahlúa over ice and float cream.

Bloody Mary
$1\frac{1}{2}$ ounces vodka
3 ounces tomato juice
$\frac{1}{2}$ t Worcestershire sauce
Dash lemon juice
2–3 drops tabasco
Salt and pepper to taste
Shake with ice and strain into old-fashioned glass over ice.

Bloody Bull
1 ounce vodka
2 ounces tomato juice
2 ounces beef bouillon
Pour over ice in highball glass, stir, add lemon squeeze and lime slice.

Desert Sunrise
$1\frac{1}{4}$ ounce vodka
$1\frac{1}{2}$ ounce Orange Juice
$1\frac{1}{2}$ ounce Pineapple Juice
1 dash grenadine
Pour over ice in tall glass, top with grenadine.

Georgia Peach
$1\frac{1}{2}$ ounce vodka
$\frac{1}{2}$ ounce peach schnapps
1 dash grenadine
Lemonade
Pour over ice in tall glass, fill with lemonade.

Harvey Wallbanger
1 ounce vodka
4 ounces orange juice
$\frac{1}{2}$ ounce galliano
Pour vodka and orange juice over ice in tall glass.
Stir, float galliano on top.

Italian Screwdriver
$1\frac{1}{2}$ ounce citrus vodka
3 ounces orange juice
2 ounces grapefruit juice
1 splash ginger ale
Mix and pour over ice into sugar rimmed parfait glass,
lime wheel garnish.

Jungle Juice
1 ounce vodka
1 ounce rum
1 ounce cranberry juice
1 ounce orange juice
1 ounce pineapple juice
$\frac{1}{2}$ ounce Triple Sec
1 splash sour mix
Pour over ice in tall glass. Garnish with orange slice
and cherry.

Long Island Iced Tea
$\frac{1}{2}$ ounce vodka
$\frac{1}{2}$ ounce gin
$\frac{1}{2}$ ounce light rum

Long Island Iced Tea (continued)
$\frac{1}{2}$ ounce tequila
Juice of $\frac{1}{2}$ lemon
1 dash cola
Pour over ice in highball glass, lemon slice garnish.

Anna's Banana
$1\frac{1}{2}$ ounce vodka
1 ounce lime juice
$\frac{1}{2}$ small ripe banana, peeled and sliced
1 t honey or orgeat
Slice lime
*Blend ingredients with ice until smooth, strain into
    cold wine glass, garnish with lime slice.*

Blue Shark
1 ounce vodka
1 ounce tequila
Few dashes Blue Curaçao
Blend or shake with ice, pour into old-fashioned glass.

Bull Shot
2 ounces vodka
4 ounces beef bouillon or consommé
$\frac{1}{2}$ ounce lemon juice
Several dashes Worcestershire sauce
Few dashes tabasco (optional)
Celery salt or horseradish (optional)
Mix with ice in cold double old-fashioned glass

Coffee Cooler
$1\frac{1}{2}$ ounces vodka
1 ounce Kahlúa
1 ounce heavy cream
4 ounces iced coffee
1 scoop coffee ice cream
*Blend or shake everything but ice cream with ice, pour
    into double old-fashioned glass, top with ice cream.*

Dubrovnik
$1\frac{1}{2}$ ounces vodka
$\frac{3}{4}$ ounce slivovitz
$\frac{1}{2}$ ounce lemon juice
$\frac{1}{2}$ t sugar syrup
Shake or blend with ice, pour into cold cocktail glass.

Fuzzy Navel
$1\frac{1}{2}$ ounces peach schnapps
Chilled orange juice
Pour schnapps into highball glass half full of ice, fill
*   with orange juice.*

Moscow Mule
2–3 ounces vodka
1 t lime juice
Ginger beer
Lime slice or wedge garnish
Stir vodka and lime juice with ice, fill with ginger beer,
*   garnish.*

Pile Driver
2 ounces vodka
3 ounces prune juice
$\frac{1}{2}$ t lemon juice
Ice
Stir well in double old-fashioned glass.

APPENDIX A

Leading U.S. Liquor Firms

Overall, the industry is shrinking because of declining sales. Bill Gates could easily buy the entire U.S. liquor industry.

There are 14 companies that could be called industry leaders. In 1997, where the most reliable recent statistics come from, there were 18 such firms, but the total was reduced by merger in 1998.

For a listing of all distillers, rectifiers, and importers of vodka (which constitutes the largest segment of liquor sales), see Chapter 3.

UDV North America/Diageo

In 1998 four of the major companies were consolidated into one, and the government ordered divestiture of some of the brands belonging to that company. Four companies which were listed as separate entities are now one, but three of their largest brands were sold to a competitor.

The merger of Grand Metropolitan and Guinness PLC into the giant UDV/Diageo, caused their subsidiaries, IDV North Americas, Schieffelin and Somerset, United Distillers USA, and Carillon Importers, to become one company. This conglomerate is now the largest liquor company in the world with 1997 sales of 22,829,000 cases, placing them at #1 in the industry with 16.5 percent market share.

The U.S. Government forced them to sell three brands, and this did somewhat lower their earnings. They sold the labels Dewar's Blended Scotch, Bombay Dry, and Bombay Sapphire Gins to Bacardi-Martini for the rumored price of 1.93 billion dollars, which moved Bacardi-Martini from the eighth largest company in earnings to the third largest, just behind Seagram America's.

UDV/Diageo now produces three gins, the #2 seller, Gordon's, with 1997 sales of 1,115,000 cases and the #10, Booth's, with sales of 100,000 cases (both domestic gins) plus the #1 import, Tanqueray, with sales of 1,350,000 cases. The company produces eight vodkas, the three largest domestics plus two more domestics, and three of the leading imports. The domestics are: #1, Smirnoff, with 5,787,000 cases sold in 1997; #2, Popov, with 2,577,000 cases; #3, Gordon's, with 1,955,000 cases; #6, Kamchatka, with 1,054,000 cases (a joint venture with Jim Beam Brands); and #16, Relska, with 316,000 cases. The imports are: #2, Stolichnaya, with 1,130,000 cases sold in 1997; #5, Tanqueray Sterling, with 175,000 cases; and #7, Priviet, with 62,000 cases.

UDV/Diageo accounts for 22.58 percent of the total gin market and 38.5 percent of the total vodka market.

Seagram Americas

Formerly the largest and now the second-largest of the U.S. liquor companies, Seagram's started in Canada and was purchased by Samuel Bronfman during the years of Prohibition. He grew it into one of the largest companies in Canada before moving the home offices into the U.S., where most of the company's business was done. Today the company is run by his sons, and controls other companies in the entertainment industry, including at least one movie studio and a major entertainment agency in California.

In 1997, the Seagram's company sold 16,828,000 cases of liquor for a market share of 12.1 percent, with earnings of $1,620,000,000, giving them a 15.3 percent share of total earnings in the spirits industry.

In the leading brands gin category, Seagram's owns the #1-seller, Seagram's Gin, with 1997 sales of 3,170,000 cases and the #9, Seagram's Lime Twist, with 1997 sales of 150,000 cases. They also import and market the fine-quality Boodles gin which did not make the leading brands list.

In the vodka category, Seagram's imports and markets the #1, Absolut, with 1997 sales of 3,440,000 cases, for a market share of 10.14 percent.

Bacardi-Martini USA

This company is best known for its dominance in the rum category. It is based in San Juan, Puerto Rico, with U.S. home offices in Miami. Bacardi was originally located in Cuba, but the family fled the country after Castro seized power and confiscated all private assets. Their move to Puerto Rico was followed by rapid and sustained growth. They became the single largest-earning brand in the industry with 1997 sales of 7,560,000 cases of rum, 57.2 percent of that category. They have now made a big push into the overall spirits market with their purchase of Dewar's Scotch, Bombay Dry gin, and Bombay Sapphire gin. With these acquisitions, Bacardi has expanded from a one-product company into a major player in the liquor industry as a whole.

With 1997 sales but with the post-1998 alignment of labels, Bacardi would be the third-largest company in the industry with sales of 19,833,000 cases for a 14.3 percent market share. In the gin category, in 1997, they would have sold 415,000 cases of Bombay Dry and Sapphire. In the vodka category, Bacardi-Martini markets their new entry Exclusiv, as either a vodka or a very light rum, but this product is not one of the leading brands and no figures for sales are currently available.

Jim Beam Brands

The fourth-largest of the major companies, it ranks #1 in the category of straight bourbon whiskey. Total sales for the company in 1997 were 15,598,000 cases for a market share of 11.2 percent and monetary earnings of $890,000,000.00.

This company represents 21 major brands including two gins and four vodkas. The gins are: #3, Gilbey's, with 1997 sales of 721,000 cases, and #13, Calvert, with sales of 82,000 cases, giving a market share of 7.05 percent of all gins sold. The vodkas are: #6, Kamchatka, which it shares with UDV/Diageo, with sales of 1,054,000 cases; #7, Wolfschmidt, with sales of 1,032,000 cases; #9, Gilbey's Vodka. with case sales of 777,000; and #24, Dark Eyes, with sales of 145,000 cases, giving a total vodka market share of 7.53 percent.

Allied Domecq

Allied Domecq, created by the merger of Allied Distillers of Great Britain and the Pedro Domecq Liquor company of Spain, is the fifth largest purveyor of distilled spirits in the United States. It represents 27 leading brands, has absorbed its two subsidiaries Hiram Walker and Domecq Importers, and now operates as one company

In 1997, it sold 8,739,000 cases for a total market share of 6.3 percent and a gross sales figure of $890,000,000. Among its labels it has one leading brand of gin, Beefeater's, #2 in the import category with 640,000 nine liter cases sold in 1997 for a 5.62 percent share of the gin market, and one imported vodka, Fris Skandia', #6 in the import category with 1997 sales of 85,000 cases and a 0.38 percent share of the vodka market. Most of the company's strength is located in cordials and liqueurs, with the Hiram Walker line of cordials and seven high-quality imported liqueurs.

Brown-Forman

This Louisville, Kentucky, firm is perhaps best known for its main label of Jack Daniel's Tennessee Whiskey, the flagship of its 12 leading brand labels. It represents one imported vodka, #4, Finlandia, with 1997 sales of 245,000 cases for a market share of 0.72 percent and has no gins.

Canandaigua Brands

This parent company of Canandaigua Wine Co. and Barton Brands Inc. came in seventh in the major brands earnings race. With their home office in Canandaigua, New York, their Barton Brands subsidiary office is located in Chicago, Illinois.

In 1997 this company sold 11,929,000 cases of spirits for a market share of 8.6 percent. With 27 labels in their portfolio, they market five leading gin labels: #4, Fleischmann's, with sales of 407,000 cases; #6, Barton's, with 346,000 cases; #8, Crystal Palace, with 172,000 cases; #12, Glenmore, with sales of 96,000 cases; and #14, Skol, with 67,000 cases sold. They also handle six leading vodkas: #4, Barton's, with sales of 1,279,000 cases; #8, Skol, with 924,000 cases; #11, Fleischmann's Royal, with 595,000 cases; #13, Crystal Palace, with 502,000 cases; #18, Old Mr. Boston's, 289,000 cases; and #25 Glenmore, 120,000 cases.

They also market other labels that did not make the leading brands list: five gins (Barclay's, Mr. Boston's English Market, Mr. Boston's Riva, Pikeman, and Schenley) and four vodkas (Barclay's, Czarina, Schenley, and a flavored vodka labeled 'Kranberi'.

Heaven Hill Distilleries

Based in Bardstown, Kentucky, where their distillery is located, this company makes and markets two leading gins and three vodkas. The gins are: #5, Burnett's White Satin (365,000 cases) and #11, Aristocrat (100,000 cases). The vodkas: #10 Aristocrat (605,000 cases); #19, Burnett's (60,000 cases); #21, Heaven Hill (190,000 cases).

William Grant & Sons

This company is best known for their leading brands of Scotch Whisky: #1, Clan McGregor, a U.S.-bottled blend, plus the single-malts #2, Glenfiddich, and #5, The Balvenie,. Grant does market some gins and vodkas but none on the leading brands category list and they prefer not to disclose the names of the labels they do market.

E&J Gallo Winery

Known mainly for its dominance in wines, E&J Brandy is the #1 leading brand in that category. Gallo does not currently make or market any gins or vodkas. In 1997 they sold 1,900,000 cases of distilled spirits for a 1.4 percent market share. This of course excludes the wines marketed by this largest of the wine companies.

Rémy Amerique

This wholly-owned subsidiary of the French Cognac giant, Rémy-Martin, markets the Canadian vodka, Iceberg, which has not yet made it onto the leading brands list. In 1997, Rémy sold 605,000 cases of spirits.

Sazerac Company

Based in New Orleans, Louisiana, this company purchased the Leestown Distillery in Frankfort, Kentucky, some time ago, where they distill or manufacture all of their proprietary labels. Currently they make and market the #14 leading vodka, Taaka, with 1997 sales of 440,000 cases, and the #15, Nikolai, with 435,000 cases, plus the organic vodka, Rain, made from yellow corn organically grown on the Fizzle Flat Farm in Yale, Ohio. They did import and market Corney & Barrows Gin, but discontinued this product in 1997.

David Sherman

This company makes and markets the #20-selling brand of vodka in the U.S., Tvarski, with 1997 sales of 310,000 cases, plus the new entry, Everclear vodka. In 1997, this company sold 1,306,000 cases of spirits for a 0.9 percent share of the market.

Charles Jacquin et Cie

Currently making and marketing the #23 leading brand of vodka, Jacquin Royale, with sales of 175,000 cases, this company does offer a gin. In 1997, Jacquin sold a total of 929,000 cases for a market share of 0.7 percent.

APPENDIX B

Addresses and Phone Numbers of U.S. Companies

Adamba Imports. 585 Meserol St., Brooklyn, NY 11237. (718)628-9700. Fax: (718)628-0920. Owner: Mr. Adam Bak.

A. Hardy USA. 9501 Devon Avenue, Suite 700, Rosemount, IL 60018. (847)698-9860. Fax: (847)698-8846. Owner: Mark Levinson.

American Byelorussian Import Co. 23 Pleasant St., Suite 308, Newburyport, MA 01950. (928)499-9797.

Archer Daniels Midland. 4666 Faries Parkway, Decatur, IL 62526. (217)4124-4319.

Austin-Nichols & Co., Inc. 156 East 46th St., New York, NY 10017. (212)455-9400. Fax: (212)455-9421. Owner: Pernod-Ricard Co., France.

Bacardi-Martini USA. 2100 Biscayne Blvd., Miami, FL 33137. (305)573-8511. Fax: (305)573-0756.

Barton Incorporated: 55 East Monroe St., Chicago, IL 60603. (312)346-9200. Fax: (312)346-5354. Owner: Canandaigua Brands.

Black Prince Distillery. 691 Clifton Avenue, Clifton, NJ 07015. (201)365-2050. Fax: (201)365-0746. Owner: Star Industries, Syosset, NY.

Brown-Forman Beverages Worldwide. P.O. Box 1080, Louisville, Kentucky. (502)585-1100. Fax: (502)774-7163.

Canandaigua Wine Co. Inc. 116 Buffalo St., Canandaigua, NY 14424. (716)394-7900. Fax: (716)394-6017.

Carillon Importers. Glenpoint Center West, Teaneck, NJ 07666. (201)461-1994. Fax: (201)461-1412. Owner: UDV America/Diageo.

Charles Jacquin et Cie. 2633 Trenton Avenue, Philadelphia, PA 19125. (215)425-9300. Fax:(215)425-9438.

David Sherman Corp. 5050 Kemper Avenue, St. Louis, MO 63139. (314)772-2626. Fax: (314)772-6021.

Distillerie Stock USA. 58-58 Laurel Hill Blvd., Woodside, NY 11377. (718)651-9800. Fax: (718)651-7806.

Domecq Importers Inc. 143 Sound Beach Avenue, Old Greenwich, CT 06870. (203)637-6500. Fax: (203)637-6599. Owner: Allied-Domecq;

Dozortsev & Sons, Ltd. 2 Rector Street, Suite 1100, New York, NY 10006. (212)480-0077. Fax: (212)693-0800.

Duggan's Distillers Products. 523 Rte.303, Orangeburg, NJ 10962. (914)359-1107. Fax: (914)359-0753.

Fifth Generation Inc. 12101 Moore Road, Austin, TX 78719. (512)243-2755.

Finnish National Diistillers, Inc. 30 Rockefeller Plaza, Suite 4300, New York, NY 10012. (212)757-4440. Fax: (212)247-0368.

Frank-Lin Distilled Products Ltd. 675 North King Road, San Jose, CA 95133. (800)922-9363. Fax: (408)258-9527. Owners: Frank and Lynn Maestri.

Frank Pesce International Group Ltd. 902 Clintmoore Road, Suite 142, Boca Raton, FL 33486. (561)997-0400. Fax: (561)997-7555.

Grain Processing Company Inc. 1600 Oregon St., Muscatine, IL 52761-4265. (319)264-4265.

Guinness Import Co. 6 Landmark Square, Stamford, CT 06901. (203)323-3311. Fax: (203)359-7204. Owner: UDV/Diageo.

Heaven Hill Distilleries, Inc. 1064 Loretto Road, Bardstown, KY 40004; (502)348-3921. Fax: (502)348-0162.

Hiram Walker & Sons. 3000 Town Center, Suite 3200, Southfield, MI 48075. (248)948-6500. Fax: (248)948-8920. Owner: Allied-Domecq.

Hood River Distillers Products. 200 S.W. Market Street, Suite 1890, Portland, OR 97201. (503)227-0663.

IDV Americas (Heublein). 450 Columbus Blvd, Hartford, CT 06142. (860)702-4000. Fax: (860)702-4539. Owner: UDV/Diageo.

IDV Americas (Paddington). 1 Parker Plaza, Fort Lee, NJ 07024. (201)592-5700. Fax: (201)592-6746. Owner: UDV/Diageo.

Jim Beam Brands. 510 Lake Cook Road, Deerfield, IL 60015. (847)948-8888. Fax: (847)948-0393. Owner: Fortune Brands.

Joseph E. Seagram & Sons, Inc. 375 Park Avenue, New York, NY 10152. (212)572-7000. Fax: (212)572-7007

Kensington House. 4770 Biscayne Blvd, Suite 1480, Miami, FL 33137. (305)573-0776. Fax: (305)573-4715.

Laird & Company. 1 Laird Road, Scobeyville, NJ 97724. (908)542-0312. Fax: (908)542-2244.

Le Vecke Corporation. 10810 Inland Avenue, Mira Loma, CA 91752. (909)681-8600. Fax: (909)681-8666.

Luctor International Inc. 9410 Prototype Dr., Reno, NV 89511. (888)539-3361. Fax: (702)853-5543. Owner: David Van der Velde.

Kittling Ridge Estate Wines & Spirits. 297 S. Service Rd. Grimsby, Ontario, Canada, L3M 4E9. (905)945-9225.

M.S. Walker Inc. 20 Third Avenue, Somerville, MA 02143. (617)776-6700. Fax: (617)776-5808.

Majestic Distilling Co. 2200 Monumental Blvd, Baltimore, MD 21227. (410)242-0200. Fax: (410)247-7831.

McCormick Distilling Co. 1 McCormick Lane, Weston, MO 64098. (816)640-2276. Fax: (816)640-2402.

Midwest Grain Co. 1300 Main Street, Atchison, KS 66002. Ph: (913)367-1480.

Millennium Import Co. 25 Main Street S.E., Minneapolis, MN 55414. (612)331-6230. Fax: (612)623-1644. Owner: Phillips Beverage Co.

Montebello Brands Company. 1919 Willow Springs Road, Baltimore, MD 21222. (410)282-8800. Fax: (410)282-8809.

Niche Marketing Co. 60 E. Hanover Avenue, Suite A2, Morris Plains, NJ 07950. (201)993-8450. Fax: (201)898-0193.

Palm Bay Imports, Inc. 100 S.E. Fifth Avenue, Boca Raton, FL 33432. (561)363-9642. Fax: (561)362-7296.

Paramount Distillers, Inc. 3116 Berea Road, Cleveland, OH 44111. (216)671-6300. Fax:(216)671-2299.

Pemar Importers. 310 21st St., Manhattan Beach, CA 90266. (310)545-7133. Fax: (310)545-7813. Owner: Andy Patashnik.

Phillips Beverage Co. 25 Main St. S.E., Minneapolis, MN 55414. (612)331-6230. Fax: (612)623-1644.

Preiss Imports. P.O. Box 2172, Ramona, CA 92065. (760)789-6010. Fax: (760)789-5461. Owner: Henry Preiss.

R. & A. Imports. 984 Monument St., Suite 205, Pacific Palisades, CA 90277. (310)454-2247. Fax: (310)459-3218.

Rémy-Amerique. 1350 Avenue of the Americas, New York, NY 10019. (212)399-4200. Fax: (212)399-6909. Owner: Rémy-Martin.

Richmond Import Co. 3158 Danville Blvd, Alamo, CA 94507. (510)820-2929. Fax: (510)820-4560.

Royal Kedem Wine Corp. 420 Kent Avenue, Brooklyn, NY 11211. (718)384-2400. Fax: (718)486-8943. Owners: The Herzog family.

Sans Wine and Spirits Co. 11 Quiet Moon, Irvine, CA 92614. (949)786-5118. Fax: (949)786-7353. Owner: Lou Sans.

Sazerac Company Inc. 803 Jefferson Hwy, New Orleans, LA 70121. (504)831-9450. Fax: (504)831-2383.

Schieffelin & Somerset. 2 Park Avenue, New York, NY 10016. (212)251-8200. Fax: (212)251-8388. Owner: UDV/Diageo.

Seagram's Grain Processors Inc. P.O. Box 7, Lawrenceburg, IL 47025. (812)537-8557.

Shaw-Ross International Imp. 15900 N.W. 15th Street, Miami, FL 33169. (305)625-6561. Fax: (305)624-3778.

Sidney Frank Importing Co. Cedar Plaza, 20 Cedar Street, New Rochelle, NY 10801. (914)633-5630. Fax: (914)633-5637. Owner: Sidney Frank.

Skyy Spirits Inc. 2822 Van Ness Avenue, San Francisco, CA 94109. (415)931-2000. Fax: (415)931-5050. Owner: Maurice Kanbar.

Spirits Marque One. 3012 Maple Avenue, Suite 450, Dallas, TX 75201. (888)252-6872. Fax: (214)720-1451.

Stanley Stawski Distilling Co. 1521 Haddon Avenue, Chicago, IL 60622. (773)278-4848. Fax: (773)278-5206.

Todhunter International Inc. 222 Lakeview Dr., Suite 1500, West Palm Beach, FL 33401. (561)655-8977. Fax: (561)655-9718.

United Distillers USA. 6 Landmark Square, Stamford, CT 06901. (203)359-7100. Fax: (2034)359-7199.

United States Distillers Products. 2285 University Avenue, St. Paul, MN 55114. (612)389-4903.

White Rock Distilleries. 21 Saratoga St., Lewistown, ME 04241. (207)783-1433. Fax: (207)783-8409. Owners: The Coulombe family.

William Grant & Sons, Inc. 130 Fieldcrest Avenue, Edison, NJ 08837. (732)225-9000. Fax: (732)225-0950. Owner: Wm. Grant & Sons, U.K.

World Wide Wine & Spirit Importers, Inc. 40 Oak St., Norwood, NJ 07648. (201)784-1990. Fax: (201)784-1987.

APPENDIX C

Vodka Labels

European (Except Poland and Russia)

Absolut. Sweden (Seagram's)
Arkhi. Mongolia
Aslanov. Belgium
Black Death. England (Richmond Importers)
Blavod's Black Vodka. England
Borzoi. England
Cardinal. Netherlands (Duggan's)
Charodei. Belorussia (America Belarussian Import-Export Co. Ltd.)
Cossack. England (Not the same as 'Cossack' in the U.S.)
Cristalnaya. England (Richmond Importers)
Danzka. Denmark
Denaka. Denmark (Sazerac)
1822. France
Eesti Viin. Estonia
Elduris. Iceland
Finlandia. Finland (Brown-Forman)
French Alps. France (Integrity Wines & Spirits)
Fris Skandia. Denmark (Hiram Walker)
Fuerst Bismarck. Germany (Niche Imports)
Gorbatschow. Germany
Gorilka. Ukraine
Grant's. Scotland
Grey Goose. France (Sidney Frank Importing Co.)
Huzzar. Ireland
Hungarian Diamond Filtered. Hungary (CVI Brands)
Ikonova. France
Iskra. Belgium
Karinskaya. Scotland
Kedem. Israel (Royal Kedem Wine & Spirits)
Ketel 1. Netherlands (Nolet Spirits)
Koskenkorva. Finland
Leningrad Cowboys. Finland

Monopol. Estonia
Monopolowa. Austria
Puschkin. Germany
Rasputin. Germany
Rigalya. Latvia
Royalty. Netherlands
Selekt. England
Sergei. Scotland
Tanqueray Sterling. England (Scheffelin & Somerset)
Tindavodka. Iceland
Ursus. Netherlands
Van Hoo. Belgium (Preiss Imports)
Vikingfjord. Norway
Virgin. Scotland
Viru Valge. Estonia
Vladivar. England
Von Haupold. Spain
Zelta. Latvia

POLAND

Baltic.
Belvedere. (Millenium Import Co.)
Bielska Zytnia. (kosher)
Bols.
Chopin. (Millenium Import Co.)
CK. (Stanley Stawski Dist.)
Cracovia.
Fiddler.
Galileo.
Gnesnenia Boonekamp. (flavored)
Herszl.
Jarzebiak. (flavored)
Jazz. (Stanley Stawski Dist.)
Krakus.
Krolewska. (Kensington House)
Krupnik. (flavored; Stanley Stawski Dist.)
Lanique.
Luksusowa. (Adamba Imports)
Mysliwska. (flavored)
Nisskosher.
Original Polish. (A. Hardy USA)
Pani Twardowska.
Perfect. (kosher)

Pieprzowka. (flavored)
Polonaise. (Stanley Stawski Dist.)
Polowa.
Posejdon. (Stanley Stawski Dist.)
Prima. (kosher)
Premium. (Stanley Stawski Dist.)
Roubelof.
Soplica.
Spodka. (potato)
Starka. (aged)
Tatra. (flavored)
Tevie.
Turowa. (flavored)
U Rebeka. (kosher)
Vistula. (potato)
Wisniowka. (flavored; Stanley Stawski Dist.)
Wyborowa. (Stanley Stawski Dist.)
Zloty Keos. (kosher)
Zubrowka. (flavored; Stanley Stawski Dist.)
Extra Zytnia. (Stanley Stawski Dist.)

RUSSIA

Altai Siberian.
Cristall. (Frank Pesce)
Krepkaya.
Kremlovskaya. (Dozortsev)
Limonnaya. (Stolichnaya; UDV/Diageo)
Moskovskaya.
Okhotnichaya. (Stolichnaya; UDV/Diageo)
Pertsovka. (Stolichnaya; UDV/Diageo)
Priviet. (M. Henri Wines Ltd.)
Pshenichnaya.
Russkaya.
Sibirskaya.
Smirnoff Black. (Heublein; UDV/Diageo)
Soomskaya.
Staraya Moskva. Pemar Imports
Stolbovaya.
Stolichnaya. (Carillon; UDV/Diageo)
Tarkhuna. (flavored)
Ultraa.
Yubileynaya. (flavored)

UNITED STATES

Argent. (Star Industries)
Aristocrat. (Heaven Hill)
Aristoff.
Banker's Club. (Laird & Co.)
Barclay's. (Barton Brands)
Barton's. (Barton Brands)
Bentley's. (Majestic)
Black Watch. (Majestic)
Boord's. (Frank-Lin)
Brilliant. (White Diamond Imports)
Burnett's. (Heaven Hill)
Caldwell's. (M.S. Walker)
Classic Club. (Majestic)
Club 400. (Majestic)
Cossack. (M.S. Walker)
Cossack Light. (M.S. Walker)
Crown Russe. (Frank-Lin; Sazerac)
Crater Lake. (Bendistillery Co.)
Crystal Palace. (Barton Brands)
Danube. (LeVecke)
Dark Eyes. (Jim Beam Brands)
Deisel Neutral Grain. (CVI Brands)
Everclear Vodka. (David Sherman)
Exclusiv. (Bacardi-Martini)
Five O'Clock. (Laird & Co.)
Fleischmann's. (Barton Brands)
Gilbey's. (Jim Beam Brands)
Gordon's. (UDV/Diageo)
Heaven Hill. (Heaven Hill)
Iceberg. (Rémy-Amerique)
Jacquin's Royale. (Charles Jacquin et Cie)
Kamchatka 80. (Jim Beam Brands; UDV/Diageo)
Kamchatka 100. (Jim Beam Brands; UDV/Diageo)
Karkov. (US Distilled Products Co.)
Kasser's 51. (Laird & Co.)
Kasser's Kavlaski. (Frank-Lin)
Kimnoff. (M.S. Walker)
Kimnoff Light. (M.S. Walker)
King's Deluxe. (LeVecke)
Korski. (Paramount Distillers)
Laird's. (Laird and Co.)
Lord Baltimore. (Majestic)
Maroff Light. (Frank-Lin)

McCall's. (Montebello Brands)
McCormick. (McCormick Distilling)
Monarch. (Monarch Imports)
Mr. Boston Vodka. (Barton Brands)
Myer's. (Paramount Distillers)
Natashka.
Nikolai. (Sazerac)
Nimbus.
Odesse. (Majestic)
Paramount. (Paramount Distillers)
Peachka Peach Vodka. (McCormick)
Phillips. (Phillips Products Co.)
Popov 80. (Heublein; UDV/Diageo)
Popov 100. (Heublein; UDV/Diageo)
Pride of America. (Montebello Brands)
Prism. (LeVecke)
Rain. (Sazerac)
Relska 80. (Heublein; UDV/Diageo)
Relska 100. (Heublein; UDV/Diageo)
Rikaloff. (Majestic)
Riva. (Barton Brands)
Royal Gate.
Ruble. (M.S. Walker)
Satka. (LeVecke)
Saxony.
Schenley Superior. (Barton Brands)
Senator's Club. (Laird & Co.)
Skol. (Barton Brands)
Skyy. (Skyy Spirits)
Smiroff. (Heublein)
S. S. Pierce. (M.S. Walker)
Taaka. (Sazerac)
Taaka Platinum. (Sazerac)
Teton Glacier Potato Vodka. (World Wide Spirits)
Tito's Handmade. (Fifth Generation, Inc.)
Traveler's Club. (Majestic)
Tvarski. (David Sherman)
Vanguard. (LeVecke)
Vladimir. (Montebello Brands)
Velvet Touch. (LeVecke)
Volska. (LeVecke)
Volsky. (LeVecke)
White Tavern.
Wolfschmidt. (Jim Beam Brands)
Zelko. (Majestic)

REST OF THE WORLD

Alcohol Victoria. Mexico
Jinro. Korea
Tic-Tac. El Salvador

FLAVORED VODKAS

Absolut Citron. Sweden (Seagram)
Absolut Limonnaya. Sweden (Seagram)
Absolut Peppar. Sweden (Seagram)
Finlandia Cranberry. Finland (Brown-Forman)
Fructal. Slovenia
Gordon's Citrus. U.S. (UDV/Diageo)
Gordon's Orange. U.S. (UDV/Diageo)
Gordon's Wildberry. U.S. (UDV/Diageo)
Gnesnania Boonekamp. Poland
Kremlovskaya Chocolate. Belgium (Dozortsev)
Kremlovskaya Limonnaya. Belgium (Dozortsev)
Smirnoff Citron. Russia (UDV Diageo)
Stolichnaya Cinnamon. Russia (UDV Diageo)
Stolichnaya Coffee. Russia (UDV Diageo)
Stolichnaya Limonnaya. Russia (UDV Daigeo)
Stolichnaya Okhotnichya. Russia (UDV Diageo)
Stolichnaya Orange. Russia (UDV Diageo)
Stolichnaya Peach. Russia (UDV Diageo)
Stolichnaya Pertsovka. Russia (UDV Diageo)
Stolichnaya Raspberry. Russia (UDV Diageo)
Stolichnaya Strawberry. Russia (UDV Diageo)
Stolichnaya Vanilla. Russia (UDV Diageo)
Tarkhuna. Russia
Wyborowa Lemon. (Palm Bay Imports)
Wyborowa Orange. (Palm Bay Imports)
Wyborowa Pineapple. (Palm Bay Imports)

VODKA LIQUEURS

Keglevich Forestberries. Italy (Distillerie Stock USA)
Keglevich Lemon. Italy (Distillerie Stock USA)
Keglevich Melon. Italy (Distillerie Stock USA)
Keglevich Peach. Italy (Distillerie Stock USA)
Keglevich Strawberry. Italy (Distillerie Stock USA)
Zone Banana. Italy (R & A Imports)
Zone Lemon. Italy (R & A Imports)
Zone Melon. Italy (R & A Imports)

Zone Peach. Italy (R & A Imports)
Zone Tangerine. Italy (R & A Imports)

AQUAVITS

1. **Aalborg.** Denmark (Munson-Shaw)
2. **Linie.** Norway (U.S. Distilled Products)
3. **O.P. Anderson.** (Duggan's)
4. **Skane.** (Duggan's)

APPENDIX D

Gin Labels

UNITED STATES

Ancient Age. (Ancient Age; Sazerac)
Banker's Club. (Laird's & Co.)
Barclay's. (Barton Brands)
Barrett's. (Frank-Lin)
Barton's Extra. (Barton Brands)
Bellows.
Boord's. (Frank-Lin)
Booth's. (Diageo/UDV)
Burnett's. (Heaven Hill)
Calvert. (Barton Corp.)
Cascade Mountain. (Bendistillery)
Cossack. (Frank-Lin)
Crown Russe. (Frank-Lin)
Crystal Palace. (Barton Brands)
English Guard. (US Distilled Products)
English Market. (Barton Brands)
Five O'Clock. (Laird & Co.)
Fleischmann's. (Barton Brands)
Gilbey's. (Jim Beam Brands)
Glenmore. (Barton Brands)
Glenwood. (Frank-Lin)
Gordon's. (Diageo/UDV)
Hayes & Hunnicutt. (US Distilled Products Co.)
Jacquin's Royale. (Charles Jacquin et Cie)
Kamchatka. (Jim Beam Brands)
Kasser's 51. (Laird & Co.)
Kavlana. (Frank-Lin)
Laird's. (Laird's & Co.)
Llord's. (Frank-Lin)
Llyon's.
London Crown Light.
Lord Baltimore. (Majestic)
Martini 90°. (Frank-Lin)

McCall's. (Montebello Brands)
McCormick. (McCormick)
Meyer's. (Paramount)
Milshire.
Monogram Diluted. (Frank-Lin)
Nikolai. (Sazerac)
Odesse. (Majestic)
Paramount. (Paramount)
Parliament House.
Pikeman. (Barton Brands)
Popov. (UDV/Diageo)
Potter's. (Frank-Lin)
Red Label.
Relska. (UDV Diageo)
Rickaloff. (Majestic)
Riva. (Barton Brands)
Royal Gate.
Saxony.
Schenley. (Barton Brands)
Seagram's. (Seagram)
Seagram's Excel. (Seagram)
Senator's Club. (Laird's & Co.)
Skol. (Barton Brands)
Taaka. (Sazerac)
White Tavern.

IMPORTED

Beefeater's. England (Allied Domecq)
Bellringer 94.4°. (Frank-Lin)
Bombadier Dry. (Gil Schy)
Bombay Dry. England (Bacardi-Martini)
Bombay Sapphire. England (Barcadi-Martini)
Boodle's. England (Seagram)
Bradburn's. England (Diageo/UDV)
Cork Dry. Ireland (Austin-Nichols)
Corney & Barrows. England (Sazerac)
Horse Guard. Scotland (Preiss Imports)
Leyden Dry. Netherlands (Luctor International)
Old Raj. Scotland (Preiss Imports)
Plymouth Dry. England (Todhunter Internationl)
Schlichte Steinhager Dry Gin. Germany (Niche)
Tanqueray. England (Scheffelin & Somerset)
Tanqueray Malacca. England (Scheffelin & Somerset)

GENEVERS

Bokma. (Preiss Imports)
Bols.
De Kuyper.
Boomsma. (CVI Brands)

APPENDIX E

Dutch Distilleries

Distilleerderij Wennecker. Postbus 124, 4700 AC Roosendaal, Netherlands. Telephone: 016-5603-7850

Woltjer & Oostingh. Blijhamsterstraat 23, 9671 AT Winschoten, Netherlands. 059-701-3681

Graanbranderij De Usvogel. Kruisweg 40, 5944 EN Arcen, Netherlands. 04-703-1240

Baarle International. Postbus 103, 5110 AC Baarle-Nassau, Netherlands. 04-257-8470

Handelsvereniging W. Beijer. P. Mastebroekweg 5, 7942 JZ Meppel, Netherlands. 052-205-1841

Berghorst Hengelo. Postbus 105, 7550 AC Hengelo, Netherlands. 07-491-8568

Distilleerderij Bestnat. Schieweg 76, 2627 AN Delft, Netherlands. 01-556-0575

Bols Benelux/Distilleerderij De Bron. Postbus 247, 2700 AE Zoetermeer, Netherlands. 07-944-5445

Distillerderij Boomsma. Postbus 265, 8901 BB Leeuwarden, Netherlands. 05-813-5135

Distillerderij Brunger. Steenbakkersweg 2, 7553 EJ Hengelo, Netherlands. 07-442-9200

Koninklijke Cooymans. Postbus 630, 5000 AP Tilburg, Netherlands. 01-365-2600

Distilleerderij Dirkswager. Postbus 12, 3100 AA Schiedam, Netherlands. 010-426-4540

Van Gastel en Hoekstra/NCK. Postbus 3447, 4800 DK Breda, Netherlands. 07-622-3950

Hiram Walker Benelux/Distilleerderij J. Melchers. Postbus 142, 4870 AC Etten-Leur, Netherlands. 016-082-5111

Hooghoudt. Postbus 679, 9700 AP Groningen, Netherlands. 05-042-0000

Distilleerderij De Woorn. Atoonweg 11, 1627 DE Hoorn, Netherlands. 022-901-7175

Distilleerderij Hulsink. Postbus, 3840 BA Harderwijk, Netherlands. 034-101-2443

Distilleerderij Janssens. Pijlsteeg 37–41. 1012 HH Amsterdam, Netherlands. 020 622-5334

Wed. S. Joustra & Zn. Kleinzand 32, 8601 BH Sneek, Netherlands. 051-501-2912

Johs. de Kuyper & Zn. Postbus 62, 3100 AB Schiedam, Netherlands. 010-426-9234

Nolet/Distilleerderij-jeneverstokerij. De Dubbele Adelaar, Postbus 38, 3100 AA Schiedam, Netherlands. 010-473-6555

Ph. van Perlstein & Zn. Postbus 1, 7000 AA Doetinchem, Netherlands. 083-402-4004

Rutte's Maatschappij. Vriesestraat 130, 3311 NS Dordrecht, Netherlands. 07-813-4467

Schermer. Kliene Noord 47, 1621 JE Hoorn, Netherlands. 022 901-7777

Smidt Drankenhandel. A.H.G. Fokkerstraat 30, 9403 AP Assen, Netherlands. 059-204-2898

B. Spekhorst. Wierdensestraat 26, 7461 BG Rijssen, Netherlands. 054-801-2419

Distilleerderij H, van Toor Jzn. Markt 20–24, 3131 CR Vlaardingen, Netherlands. 010-434-2577

United Distillers Nederland. Verhoeven, Postbus 2083, 5001 CB Tilburg, Netherlands. 01-358-0111

UTO Nederland. Postbus 14, 3100 AA Schiedam, Netherlands. 010-473-1088

V/d Valk & Co. Postbus 61, 2250 AB Voorschoten, Netherlands. 07-161-7242

A. H. Wanders/Distilleerderij Onder de Boompjes. Hagastraat 131–135, 3114 NC Schiedam, Netherlands. 010-426-4285

C. van Wees/Distilleerderij De Ooievaar. Driehoekstraat 10, 1015 GL Amsterdam, Netherlands. 020-626-4072

APPENDIX F

Gin and Vodka Association of Great Britain

Alcohols Limited. Charrington's House, The Causeway, Bishop's Stortford, Hertfordshire CM23 3EW, England. Telephone: 01-27-965-8464

Barber Kingsland. Wines & Spirits Division, Fairhills Road, Irlam, Manchester M30 6BD, England. 0161-775-8431

Burn Stewart Distillers plc. 8 Milton Road, College Milton North, East Kilbride G74 5BU, Scotland. 0135-526-0999

Coates and Co. (Plymouth) Ltd. Black Friars Distillery, Southside Street: Plymouth, Devon PL1 2LQ, England. 0175-266-5292

The Greenall Group plc. Causeway Distillery, Warrington, Cheshire WA4 6RH, England. 0192-565-0111

Greenwich Distillers Ltd. Thamesbank House, Tunnel Avenue, Greenwich, London SE10 0PA, England. 0181-853-7341

Halewood International Ltd. Wilson Road, Huyton, Merseyside L36 6AD, England. 0151-480-8800

Hayman Ltd. 70 Eastways Park, Witham, Essex CM8 3YE, England. 0137-651-7517

Highland Distillers plc. West Kinfauns, Perth PH2 7XZ, Scotland. 0173-844-0000

Ian MacLeod and Co. Ltd. Russell House, Dunnet Way, Broxburn, Edinburgh EH52 5BU, Scotland. 0150-685-2205

Inver House Distillers Ltd. Moffat Distilleries, Airdrie, Lanarkshire ML6 8PL, Scotland. 0123-676-9377

JBB (Greater Europe) plc. Dalmore House, 310 St Vincent St., Glasgow G2 5RG, Scotland. 0141-248-5771

James Burroughs Ltd. 60 Montford Place, Kennington Lane, London, SE11 5DF, England. 0171-820-4200

John Grant (Blenders) Ltd. 7 Laigh Road, Catrine, Ayrshire KA5 6SQ, Scotland. 0129-055-1211

Lichfield Gin Co. Independence House, 84 Lower Mortlake Street, Richmond, Surrey TW9 2HS, England. 0181-332-1188

London Gin Co. 8 Windward House, Plantation Wharf, London SW11 3TU, England. 0171-223-5723

London and Scottish Spirits Ltd. Meadow View House, Tannery Lane, Gosden Common, Bramley, Guildford, Surrey, England. 0148-389-4650

The Original Black Vodka Company Ltd. 202 Fulham Road, London SW10 9NB, England. 0171-352-2096

Pierre Smirnoff. 8 Henrietta Place, London W1M 9AB, England. 0171-518-5500

Seagram (UK) Ltd. The Ark, 201 Talgarth Road, Hammersmith, London, W6 8BN, England. 0181-250-1801

Tanqueray, Gordon and Co. Ltd. Landmark House, Hammersmith, London W6 9DP, England. 0181-846-8040

UDV UK. Templefields House, River Way, Harlow, Essex CM20 2EA. 0127-962-6801

Virgin Spirits Ltd. Independence House, 84 Lower Mortlake Road, Richmond, Surrey, England; 0181-332-1188

William Grant and Sons Ltd. Customer Service Centre, Phoenix Centre, Strathclyde Business Park, Motherwell ML4 3AN, Scotland. 0169-884-3843

Short
Bibliography

Stephen Bayley. *Gin: A Private Publication by the Gin and Vodka Association of Great Britain*. London, 1994.

Desmond Begg. *The Vodka Companion: A Connoisseur's Guide*. Philadelphia: Running Press, 1998.

Barnaby Conrad III. *The Martini: An Illustrated History of an American Classic*. San Francisco: Chronicle Books, 1995.

John Doxat. *The Gin Book*. London: Quiller Press, 1989.

Lowell Edmunds. *Martini, Straight Up: The Classic American Cocktail*. Baltimore: Johns Hopkins University Press.

Nicholas Faith and Ian Wisniewski. *Classic Vodka*. London: Prion Books, 1997.

Neil M. Heyman. *Russian History*. McGraw-Hill, 1993.

William Pokhlebkin. *A History of Vodka*. English translation by Renfrey Clark. New York: Verso/New Left Books, 1992. Original Russian publication, 1991.

Pattie Lee Vargas and Richard Dale Gulling Jr. *Cordials from Your Kitchen*. Pownal, Vermont: Storey Publishing, 1997.

Index